Renewing Christianity

Dedicated to my sister Lois and her husband Tim, who were often in my thoughts as I wrote.

James H. Hindes

Renewing Christianity

Anthroposophic Press

First published in 1995 by Floris Books and
in 1996 by Anthroposophic Press

Published by Anthroposophic Press
RR 4 Box 94A1, Hudson, NY 12534

Front cover picture: *Ascension* by Ninetta Sombart
Back cover picture: *Journey to Emmaus* by Max Wolfhügel

ISBN 0–88010–390–6

Printed in Great Britain

Contents

Foreword

I haver tried to keep this book on Rudolf Steiner's contribution to Christianity short yet plausible. Brevity with Steiner, as with any true revolutionary, can often cause him to sound either bizarre or trite. My intention has been to help the reader avoid premature judgments concerning the origins of Steiner's ideas or the destination of the spiritual path he follows. How well I have succeeded, others will have to decide.

Of the many people whom I would like to thank for their help, my wife Cynthia must be listed first. She carefully read every draft with red pencil in hand and was always available to provide a quick 'objective reader's' response to a paragraph, page or chapter thrust into her otherwise occupied hands. Sanford Miller's trenchant and insightful comments on early drafts of the manuscript helped me with clarity and in some places to avoid saying things I did not intend. Paul Margulies and Christopher Bamford, with their careful reading and lively discussion on the themes of the book provided invaluable encouragement. I would also like to thank my editor, Christopher Moore, whose guidance has kept the book focused on the original intention of brevity and readability.

When writing and publishing a book today every author and editor must confront the problem of 'inclusive language.' Every solution will involve compromises that disappoint some, please others and enrage a few. The readers of this book will see the choices I have made. 'Mankind' has largely been eliminated but the masculine third person generic has, for the most part, been retained. Some of my reasons for these decisions are found in Chapter 5 on gender questions in religion.

James H. Hindes
Advent, 1995

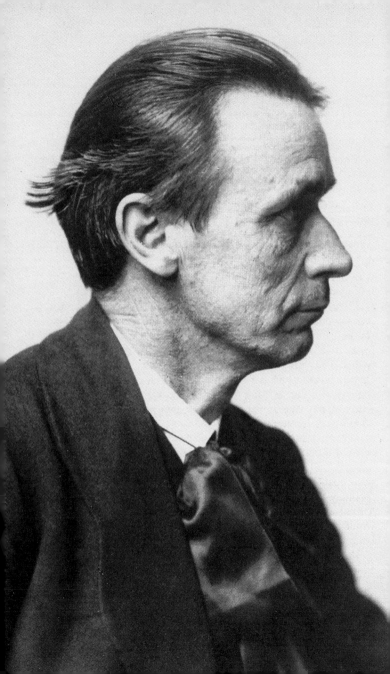

Introduction

The phone rang in the late afternoon. A young woman who had found our number in the telephone book was on the line. Our name, The Christian Community, sounded friendly to her and she felt the need for friends. She was scheduled the next day for an abortion and told me she wanted to discuss her decision with a minister. I told her to come right over and we would talk.

Later I discovered she was twenty-four years old, that this was to be her third abortion in three years and that there was no 'father' in the picture. She admitted to enjoying life to the utmost and hoping to continue doing so. The former abortions bothered her only late at night when she had trouble sleeping. But she knew that having a baby now would interfere with the life she wanted to lead. Nevertheless, she was now having second thoughts about having yet another. She was in a state of complete indecision.

My task, as I saw it, was to help her make a decision as consciously as possible in light of all the knowledge she could muster. In other words, to help her to act as responsibly as she was capable. Ultimately, the decision had to be hers, of course, for she would bear most of the consequences, physical, psychological and spiritual. Any mistake had to be hers. Only then would she have a chance to learn from it. It is a rare human being indeed who can learn from the mistakes of others.

However, I soon realized that she wanted something that I could not give her. She expected a Christian priest to tell her what to do. Then she could either dutifully follow instructions

Rudolf Steiner in 1916

or, more likely in this case, rebel against perceived authority. Either way she would no longer be responsible. All too often people try to pin me down as to exactly what my advice is: 'What would a Christian do in my situation, Rev Hindes?' I usually answer: 'Well, what do you want to do, and why?' Christ has a special, individual relationship to the 'I' of every human being. I firmly believe that anyone striving to act out of his true 'I,' that is, do what he or she really wants to do, will be guided by higher powers, ultimately to Christ himself.

Should she have the abortion? The answer to that question depends on the answers to many other questions. A short list might begin with: What is an abortion? What is a human being? Where do we come from? Where do we go after death? Do we reincarnate? If so, do we choose our parents? What is destiny, fate or karma? What is pain or pleasure really? Who am I and what am I becoming? What gives my life meaning?

The Bible would seem to have answers to some of these questions. But the Bible presupposes answers to many questions that are not at all that clear to many people today: How do I know anything? What or whom can I trust? What is consciousness? What is real? What is a dream? How can I tell the difference?

To help this woman with her decision I sought to explore some of these questions, to help her become clear in her mind about things she might have known unconsciously but needed help remembering: values and perspectives that she could feel in her heart as true were raised to thought. She needed true knowledge; not instructions or even 'information.' (It is just because information without values is meaningless and confuses that it is used by those who seek to manipulate us.) But true knowledge, which can only be a personal experience, is the basis for decisions, which, even when wrong, can lead us to act out of depths of soul where Christ speaks to us in a voice which is our own.

However, to reach those depths of soul we need the willingness to take responsibility for our actions and the courage to think new thoughts. In order to help the woman make a decision based on knowledge I tried to find out what she thought about the big questions and to introduce a few new ideas that might open new perspectives. Had she had the time I would have explained a new Christian world view to her. This present book contains much of what would then have been said.

I believe that we are always responsible for our actions, whether or not our thoughts are clear concerning our intentions. Therefore, to accept responsibility for our actions we must begin by taking responsibility for our thoughts, by striving to be conscious and courageously thinking and evaluating new ideas and perspectives.

Our desperate times and lives are driving many people to think again about religion, to adopt a religious perspective. Some simply take on Christian fundamentalism with its stress on basic biblical commandments and promises. Obedience is usually their highest virtue. Others regard Christianity as fundamentally outdated and look to other philosophies, usually Eastern and/or ancient. Transcendence is often their highest virtue.

In the work of Rudolf Steiner I myself found an approach that allowed me to think and feel like a modern spiritually autonomous human being, and simultaneously to understand the deep truth of Christianity. I will be eternally grateful to Rudolf Steiner's works for having introduced me to a Christianity that can be thought and to a living Christ who can be found and experienced today. He showed me that Jesus of Nazareth was the Son of God who died on the cross and was resurrected as Christ Jesus, the saviour of all humankind. Indeed, spiritual science, or anthroposophy, shows that the meaning of human history can only be found through an understanding of the death and Resurrection of Jesus Christ.

But Steiner was not a theologian in any ordinary sense and has been largely ignored by professionals. His starting point, rather than the examination and analysis of ancient sacred texts, was radically different. He began with an examination of spiritual realities through his conscious, direct perception in those spiritual realities. In some quarters of late it has become more acceptable to be a visionary or mystic. However, such an approach is often rejected by churches as a subversion of faith, and at the same time is also viewed as unscientific. The general public, following the lead of the scientific establishment, reserves the word 'science' for the exploration and mastery of the physical world. It believes that the only real sciences are the 'hard sciences.' Steiner pointed out that this unconscious and unjustified assumption is as wrong as it is widespread. As any philosopher of science will admit, it is the *method*, not the subject matter that determines whether any given investigation is scientific.

Steiner's research into higher spiritual worlds was scientific in method, repeatable and verifiable. However, the exercises required to develop the faculties needed for spiritual investigations are rigorous, demanding and require years of consistent application before one can verify or contest Steiner's results with modern clairvoyance. Those who have made those efforts have begun to verify Steiner's work. Those who do not possess such faculties naturally tend not to believe in their existence. At the same time much of Steiner's work has yielded results eminently practical in the earthly realm, in agriculture, medicine and in education to name just a few.

The results of Steiner's investigations are consistent internally and also when placed alongside the actual facts presented to us by the physical world. Of course, Steiner's descriptions do not always harmonize with the *theories* of modern science. And since we do not always realize the extent to which our 'facts' about the physical world have actually been created by our theories, there is sometimes an *apparent* conflict.

Another facet of Rudolf Steiner which is of fundamental importance for understanding his views on Christianity ought to be mentioned at the outset. He was a thoroughly modern man. This is made evident by two personal needs which accompanied his life and work as recurring themes. The first was his need for *spiritual autonomy*, that is, the need to decide for himself about the truth of reality and not be told by any external authority, be it a book, tradition or institution. His writings and lectures were the results of his own direct spiritual investigations and not any eclectic synthesis of wisdom traditions from ancient or modern sources. Secondly, he needed to understand *through thinking* the things that presented themselves to him in

life. As modern human beings we orient ourselves today primarily through our thinking.

This book is not about Steiner's path of meditation, the path
leading to initiation and direct experience of the supersensory
world. His own books provide the best introduction for those
interested. This book is concerned with those results of Steiner's research which shed light on the Christian religion.

Many today say and feel that life has no meaning. Everything seems relative; meaning depends upon what one person-
ally wishes to believe. Yet the denial of any structure to 'being'
or 'existence' is like a rejection of the idea of north and south.
If we lack a compass to tell us where the north and south poles
are located we can easily stop believing that any such polarity
rules the earth. The compass the human soul needs in order to
find meaning in life is a relationship to the spiritual world
which is both *conscious* and *living*. The previous evolution of
human consciousness has brought us to the point where this
awareness of the spirit, this living relationship to spiritual beings has faded away. Instead we have developed both individual
freedom and the ability to think abstractly.

Our task now is to retain the freedom while re-enlivening
our experience of spiritual beings. Here the wealth of concrete
images, pictures and concepts of the spiritual world found in
Rudolf Steiner's work can help us with this desperately needed
re-thinking and re-visioning of reality that will enable us again
to possess such a compass.

Modern theologies ask whether Christianity has any significance for the present and future above and beyond its obvious
ethical and humanitarian impulses. At the same time, many
people today experience a longing for an expansion of consciousness, for authentic supersensory experience. They want to
find a relationship to Christ, not only the Christ who founded
a historical religion, but also to the Christ who is a living spirit
who can help us in our present need.

The work of Rudolf Steiner offers many approaches to
answer this question. Standing outside the theatre of theological
debate in our time, Steiner begins with a detailed experience of
the whole. His descriptions of the deeds of spiritual beings are

straightforward and concrete. To many, they appear like odd shaped pieces which do not fit into the accepted puzzle being worked on by contemporary theologians. However, when placed together they result in a vision of reality which is entirely whole, comprehensive and concrete.

For the most part modern theologians have simply ignored these descriptions. To them Steiner appears to be speaking of another universe. But perhaps that is just what is needed, a universe envisioned completely and deeply enough to offer radically new perspectives on the questions which trouble modern life and the often painful decisions it demands of us.

1. Steiner's approach to religion

A citizen of two worlds

From one point of view, Rudolf Steiner had a relationship to religion similar to that of many contemporaries. He received religious instruction at school and attended church as a child but his connection with the church ended before his fourteenth birthday. His religious teachers could not answer his deepest questions concerning the meaning of life and human existence. He turned to natural science, a field in which he found people who appeared unafraid to ask questions. In the religion of his time he saw resigned devotion to revelations of the past and inappropriate claims to power. He read and listened to theologians but to him they seemed lost in a fabric of abstractions, separated from the everyday experience of living human beings.

But from another point of view Steiner's relationship to religion was quite unique. For already as a small child he had a living experience of spiritual beings in a spiritual world. Belief in God or a higher world was never a question of faith for Steiner. His problem as a child was rather to discover how the spiritual world and the everyday physical world were related. In his autobiography he describes his joy at having found in mathematics a subject that belonged equally in both worlds. Concerning geometry he said:

> That one can live within the mind in the shaping of forms perceived only within oneself, entirely without impression upon the external senses, became for me the deepest satisfaction. I found in this solace for the unhappiness which my unanswered questions had caused me ...

I said to myself: The objects and occurrences which the senses perceive are in space. But, just as this space is outside man, so there exists within man a sort of soul-space which is the scene of action of spiritual beings and occurrences. I could not look upon thoughts as something like images which the human being forms of things; on the contrary, I saw in them revelations of a spiritual world on this field of action in the soul. Geometry seemed to me to be a knowledge which appears to be produced by man, but which nevertheless, has a significance quite independent of him. ... I felt that one must carry knowledge of the spiritual world within oneself after the manner of geometry.[1]

The riddle presented to Steiner by his living in two different worlds led him to study mathematics and natural science at a technical college while pursuing a philosophic search in his spare time. He felt he 'must grapple with nature' in order to understand the world of spirit which confronted him in 'self-evident perception.'[2]

I felt duty bound at that time to seek for the truth through philosophy. I had to study mathematics and natural science. I was convinced that I should find no relation with them unless I could place their findings upon a solid foundation of philosophy. But I beheld a spiritual world *as reality*. In perfectly clear vision the spiritual individuality of everyone was manifest to me. This had in the physical body, and in action in the physical world, merely its expression. It united itself with that which came as a physical germ from the parents. The dead human being I followed on his way into the spiritual world.[3]

Already at age eight he had experienced the departed soul of a relative who had just taken her own life. He knew at that time that she had died and was in the spiritual world. He understood what she was saying to him and knew that he could speak to no

*Johann
Wolfgang
von Goethe
(1749–1832)*

one about the experience. He was alone with his gift of natural, spontaneous clairvoyance.

He realized that he knew spiritual facts and physical facts. His question was 'how?' In the scientific writings of Johann Wolfgang von Goethe he found an approach to knowing nature very much like his own. In 1882, at age twenty-one, the task of editing, and writing introductions to, *The Scientific Writings of Goethe* in *Kürschners National Literatur* edition was given to Steiner.

The fruits of this work were published in *Goethe the Scientist* (1884–97) and *A Theory of Knowledge Based on*

Goethe's World Conception (1886). These works display a
selfless devotion to the ideas and methods Goethe employed in
understanding nature. They also enabled Steiner to investigate
a thinker who seemed to have developed a preliminary form of
clairvoyance. Goethe's ability to see the spiritual reality behind
plants was not unlike the clairvoyance Steiner himself possessed
since childhood yet had been unable to tell anyone about. By
the time the Goethe volumes for which he was responsible were
all published, Steiner was generally recognized as the leading
expert on Goethe's scientific writings.

*Rudolf Steiner
in 1891.*

Early pronouncements on Christianity

As a well known and respected figure in the cultural life of Weimar and Berlin, Steiner published a prodigious amount on philosophical, literary and cultural themes during the two decades from 1880 to 1900. In all this writing he often said things critical of Christianity. Because of the way he spoke of Christ after 1900 he was accused of inconsistency. Yet he never renounced any of his earlier writings. He explained why in his autobiography:

> When I used the word 'Christianity' at that time [before 1900], I had in mind the doctrine of the Beyond which was in force in the Christian creeds. The whole content of religious experience referred to a world of spirit which was supposed not to be attainable by man in the unfolding of his spiritual powers. What religion has to say, what it has to give as moral precepts, was supposed to be derived from revelations which come to man from without. Against this idea my view of the spirit was opposed, maintaining that the world of spirit is experienced precisely as is the sense-world in what is perceptible in relation to man and to nature. My ethical individualism also was opposed to this idea, maintaining that the moral life proceeds, not from without in the form of commandments obeyed, but from the unfolding of the human soul and spirit, wherein lives the divine.[4]

And on the next page we read:

> Before this [the appearance of the book *Christianity as Mystical Fact*] the Christian content to which I referred had always been that found in the existing creeds. ... The Christianity which I had to seek I did not find anywhere in the creeds.

Steiner's epistemology

Steiner always asserted the continuity of his development. For him, modern scientific methodology and spiritual subject matter are completely compatible. *The fabric of science and spirituality is seamless.* His answer to the epistemological question, How do I know anything? is independent of the 'thing' investigated. Knowledge of nature presupposes knowledge of the self who does the knowing. So too, knowledge of God must begin with self-knowledge.

A complete description of Steiner's epistemology would exceed the limits of this little book. In Steiner's doctoral dissertation of 1892 we find the shortest account. A full translation of the German title shows Steiner to be in step with contemporary German academia: *The Fundamental Problem of the Theory of Knowledge with particular Reference to Fichte's Philosophy. Prolegomena to the Reconciliation of the Philosophical Consciousness with Itself.*[5] However, his book, *The Philosophy of Freedom* (1894) contains perhaps the most complete account including consequences.

Steiner explains how Immanuel Kant (1724–1804) began with the idea that our ability to know is inextricably bound up with the way our senses are organized. Kant maintains that 'concepts without perception are empty' and any perception other than of the physical world is not known to ordinary consciousness. Steiner disagrees. He claims that we already participate in a spiritual world *through the concepts we think* — concepts are *not* derived from sense experience. The idea of a straight line does not come from the physical world. We are able to recognize straight things because the idea, a non-physical thing, lives within us. Concepts do not come from seeing the physical world but from an 'inner seeing.' Steiner calls this kind of perception, as distinct from sense perception, intuition. With concepts we are intuitively in touch with a supersensory world. It is true that when we perceive sensible objects our senses provide input from the sensible world, but it is the concept that allows us to know what we are seeing. Our

*Immanuel
Kant
(1724–1804)*

activity, which usually goes unnoticed, consists in the addition of the concept. This we call thinking. Higher reflective thinking obviously requires searching for concepts but so, too, does simple seeing.

Through a conscious strengthening and enhancing of this thinking activity (so that it no longer needs the foundation of the physical senses) it is possible to attain to knowledge of supersensory reality. The contents of knowledge are immediately given to us without any mediation of the senses. The world of supersensory beings and their deeds are then step-wise revealed to us in our consciousness where, in the act of knowing, concept and percept are one.

Thinking itself is the first 'supersensory object' to be grasped in this way. Personal experience, direct and immediate, of the clarity and spiritual substance of the act of thinking conveys to us the certainty of knowledge. To begin with, this clarity applies only to our thinking about the concrete activity of thinking. The individual through his thinking activity

'observes' himself in action, that is, in thinking. This activity
then requires no further qualification or characterization through
concepts because it is immediately transparent to itself. The
only 'content' that is here grasped is the activity of thinking
itself. *It is the thinking 'I' that is both the place where thinking
occurs and the agent actively thinking.* Thus the usual subject-
object split created by thinking is negated.

Supersensory knowledge

The next step, in Steiner's own words, is: 'We can grasp thinking by means of itself. The question is, whether we can also
grasp anything else through it.'[6]
    Supersensory reality cannot be deduced from concepts. Kant
was correct about that. However, once we have attained pure
thinking free from the sense world, thinking in which percept
and concept are united, what then appears to human consciousness? If, as Steiner says, reality is a unity which is then split by
our human senses into two halves, the sensible world around us
and the thinking that takes place in our minds, then there must
also be some content that will appear to pure thinking. But the
nature of such content *cannot be determined by theorizing.* Only
the actual *praxis* of supersensory knowing can then determine
what I experience. Such a *praxis* of knowing is described by
Steiner in many books, for example, *Knowledge of the Higher
Worlds and Its Attainment.*
    In his own life this *praxis* led him increasingly to deepen his
knowledge of Christianity. However, as noted earlier, there is
an apparent contradiction between his earlier and later pro-
nouncements concerning Christianity. In his autobiography he
discusses his development saying:

> The Christianity which I had to seek I did not find any-
> where in the creeds. After the time of testing had sub-
> jected me to stern battles of the soul, I had to submerge
> myself in Christianity and, indeed, in the world in which
> the spiritual speaks thereof. ... It was during the time

when I made the statements about Christianity so opposed in literal content to later utterances that the true substance of Christianity began germinally to unfold within me as an inner phenomenon of knowledge.[7]

This 'phenomenon of knowledge' was a mystical experience having the transparent clarity of modern thinking. It was an *experience* of knowledge, an experience which, since the time of the Church Fathers, had been declared to be possible only as a 'mystical feeling' occurring in that part of the soul where faith takes place. Steiner then described this knowledge in the language of western mysticism. His book, *Mysticism at the Dawn of the Modern Age* praises and discusses the achievements of Meister Eckhart, Johannes Tauler, Jacob Boehme and Angelus Silesius. He also points out that their mysticism lacked the power to survive into the future because they had sought to reach the spirit of the universe without first training their thinking in natural science.

*Jakob Boehme
(1515–1624)*

*Angelus
Silesius
(Johannes
Scheffler,
1624–77)*

In his epistemological works he shows how reality, seen both
from the physical and spiritual sides, arises in the human self,
the I, in self-consciousness, through the activity of knowing. He
sees two chief dangers on the path to the spirit: mysticism and
materialistic natural science. Mysticism is the temptation to
achieve spiritual experience without keeping one's thinking
united with and 'grounded in' the foundations provided by the
physical world. Our consciousness first awakens in the physical
world of objects. Because our perceiving and thinking are constantly corrected by physical reality we are schooled in objectivity. *We must not lose what we have so attained.* Materialistic
natural science employs such thinking but forgets thinking's
origin in the conscious human I and therefore unconsciously
insinuates a total separation of the human self from nature.

In sum, Rudolf Steiner developed a philosophical basis for
the scientific study of all aspects of reality, both esoteric and
exoteric. Where in the past one was only permitted to exercise
faith with regard to spiritual, supersensory ideas, now in our

time *knowledge* is also possible. Steiner himself followed this path of knowledge and described the results of his researches as well as the path itself, that others may find the way into this *praxis*. His claim that the path to knowledge of higher worlds leads to knowledge that is scientific and verifiable will not concern us any further. It is important to bear in mind only that Steiner's sources were neither traditional nor historical. Neither was he a medium for some purported 'guide' to speak to humanity. He based his method on the consciousness of the human being free from any external sources of coercion, be they from the dogmatism of materialism or the dogmatism of revelation. Nevertheless, he also said that studying the results of spiritual-scientific investigations, that is, reading his books and transcriptions of his lectures as well as other true descriptions of the spiritual world, could also serve as a means to begin following the path. He did not wish for any act of faith in his revelations. He asked only that others *think* them as clearly as possible and without preconceived ideas. Merely thinking a true thought will have its effects on the soul. Although it is true that others sometimes use Steiner's descriptions as a new form of revelation, we must remember that was not his intention.

2. Our place in space and time

The human being

According to Rudolf Steiner the human being should not be
divided into two parts, one heavenly and the other earthly. *Body*
and *spirit* are constantly influencing each other through a third
entity, the *soul*. The body can influence what we feel in our
soul and hence our spiritual life. But it is also true that spiritual
ideals can inspire our souls and hence lead us to act with our
bodies in the physical world. This threefold division of the
human being is supplemented by a fourfold division consisting
of the I, the astral body, the etheric body and the physical body,
each of which has a spiritual, soul and bodily aspect.[8]

What is the human physical body? Strictly speaking we see
it only after death when the life forces that have permeated it
have withdrawn. During life the physical body is the spatial
arena where forces of life are constantly taking in, transforming
and then giving up the substances of nature. The living organism maintains its form during this constant exchange of mineral
substances. Rudolf Steiner's supersensory perception saw the
physical, material body permeated by a pattern of forces which
actually forms and shapes the physical body in all its details.
This pattern he recognized as a being or 'body' independent of
the physical body. It is both the 'architect' of the physical body
and the life of the body. It can be called the 'body of formative
forces,' the 'life body,' or the 'etheric body.' Life forces are
neither physical nor psychic. They cannot be measured with
physical instruments; neither can they be characterized by any
all-encompassing nebulous concept called 'spirit.' They are a
specific kind of spiritual force called etheric because of their

region of origin within the spiritual world. They have a corresponding kinship with the kingdom of the plants, that is, with growth and regeneration.

The physical and life bodies together provide the basis for the soul or psychic life, which then, in turn, provides the basis for our spiritual life. The lowest parts of the soul life we can see in the animal kingdom which is the next step up from the plant world. Everything which constitutes the life of the plant is found again in the animal kingdom: formative forces of growth, regeneration and reproduction. The first thing that goes beyond plants is mobility. This is a manifestation of the presence of yet higher forces. Reacting to stimuli, both inner and outer, the animal attempts to move toward or away from something. This movement is caused by emotion (the word itself indicates this) or feelings. The feelings and consciousness of bodily pleasure and pain are the most basic and primitive expressions of soul life. This soul element which is still attached to the body, which sits in all our members, so to speak, and feels itself *in* the body and *as* body, Rudolf Steiner calls the 'soul body' or 'astral body.' The last term refers to that region of the spiritual world where it originates.

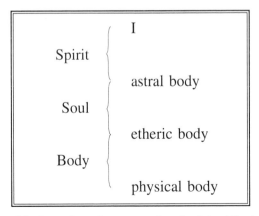

The astral body mediates between soul and spirit while the etheric body connects the body with the soul.

Life in the etheric world of biological forms unfolds in the polarity of life and death, while life in the astral world unfolds between the poles of attraction and repulsion, sympathy and antipathy, pain and pleasure. But the astral body is the origin of more than emotions and feelings. Thinking and willing in their most basic forms also have their basis in the astral body. There must, of course, be a stimulus for feelings and will impulses to arise. Perception occurs when we create an idea or inner image from an external stimulus. The most basic form of thinking is the result of an external stimulus being translated into impressions and images which are then combined in the soul. With the eye this is obvious but it holds true for other senses as well. This basic form of thinking uses symbols to re-create the external world in the mind, thus creating the foundation necessary for all higher thinking.

The step from the involuntary association of one mental picture with another to the conscious formation of concepts and judgments requires the presence of the fourth 'member' of the human being: the I. Steiner understood this word in the neutral, philosophical sense, according to which the human being is that being having *consciousness of self.* Hence the simplicity of the word I, which points to the centre of our conscious experience of self. Complicating the picture is the fact that there *is* a sense in which it is correct to say that 'I am my body;' but it is not true to say that the I, the conscious centre of the human being is merely the product of the body. Steiner taught that an eternal, indestructible being, the human I, lives and is manifested within and through the body. When properly understood this I — its purpose, history and possibilities — is the key to the entire meaning of human existence. But we would never have been able to know this without our physical bodies. Human self-consciousness requires, to begin with, incarnation in a body.

It is impossible to understand Steiner's conception of Christianity without understanding his concept of the I. It is not sufficient merely to say that the I is consciousness of self. Only because I *am* an 'I' can I have a consciousness of self. And only because I have an astral body, with its inner life, is it possible for my I to become conscious of itself. But the astral body

Johann Gottlieb Fichte (1762–1814)

is only reactive. The I is active out of itself. Before Steiner the German philosopher Johann Gottlieb Fichte (1762–1814) discovered this essential characteristic of the I: 'That whose being or essence consists simply in the fact that it posits itself as existing, is the self ...' and 'What was I then before I came to self-consciousness? The natural reply is: *I* did not exist at all; for I was not a self. The self exists only insofar as it is conscious of itself.' And, 'The self is that which it posits itself to be; and it posits itself as that which it is.'[9] There is nothing in the I that has not come out of the I itself. The I is the origin of everything that lives within it. Of course, the I is influenced by the not-I which includes other I-beings with which it is in contact. Nevertheless, nothing enters the essential human I which is not consciously allowed in. However, what is allowed in, that is, into our consciousness, is *re-created* in the self and thereby becomes the property, the possession of the I. Expressed most starkly, Steiner would say with Fichte that the I, the self, does not really exist except when it is constantly creating itself anew

through its own inner activity. The I cannot be thought of in the
same way as anything else, be it mineral, plant or animal. It is
not a thing but an activity like a spiritual fire.

Our will also comes forth from our I, but here it is difficult
to distinguish between higher impulses of will and wants and
desires which rise up unconsciously from our other bodies.
Obviously, the will that comes from the physical body does not
necessarily belong to the I even though we become conscious
of it in 'the same place' where the I becomes self-conscious.
The act of distinguishing with our thinking in this realm is what
can make us free. Nothing outside the I can make it free or
unfree. Only the individual I can decide for itself if it is to be
free or not.

The interaction between body, soul, and spirit can only be
understood when all three 'bodies' and the I are taken into
account. According to Steiner the physical body is the means by
which the purely spiritual can appear in the earthly realm of
matter; it can be either a prison for the I or its instrument,
depending on the development of the soul. The Platonic dualism
of body and soul is overcome by this conception which sees the
purely spiritual I united with its polar opposite, matter, through
the complex interactions of the astral, etheric and physical
aspects of our bodily nature.

Created by God, the human being has the divine power to
create because he, himself, is like God, an I-being with the
concomitant self-consciousness of an I-being. As we have
briefly indicated, the possibility of freedom rests upon this very
self-consciousness. And without freedom there can be no love,
neither love of God nor love of one's fellow human being. In
creating the human being, God's own deed of love was to leave
a free space in our hearts where the human I can awaken and
then decide for itself what it wants to do. God respects this
space and does not force himself upon us. There are, of course,
other beings who want to do this; they will be discussed later
in this chapter.

Selfhood and the possibility of true freedom are what is
meant by our being created 'in the image of God' (Genesis
1:26f). The power to be free is found only in an I. Like the tiny

flame of divine fire described by Meister Eckhart, the human
I, as described by Steiner, is an eternal light; it is pure spirit, a
part of God himself. Yet this is not to say that the human being
is God anymore than to say that a drop of water *is* the ocean
merely because they are of the same substance.

The human being with his four members does not develop
in a vacuum. He exists on and through the earth. Before con-
tinuing with Steiner's description of the human being and
human evolution it is necessary to give a sketch of his account
of the origin of the universe itself.

The universe

Where did the universe and with it the earth and humankind
come from? Traditional Christian theology points to God, who
has the power of self-creation, and says the answer is to be
found in the first chapter of Genesis. On the other hand, modern natural science speaks of a 'Big Bang' which presupposes
the existence of energy and matter, millions of years in the past.
The two accounts have one thing in common: their conception
of matter as the solid stuff of modern day experience. Both
accept the law of the conservation of matter, science explicitly,
theology implicitly. A modern theologian would hardly dare
question the eternal nature of atoms assumed by modern
physics and chemistry. Rudolf Steiner does. He sees matter as
a 'densification' of spirit and describes in many places and in
detail the stages that matter has evolved through. Furthermore,
in the future it will again gradually evolve back into a state of
pure spirit. Not only has human consciousness evolved; the
'stuff' of the universe is itself actually involved in a process of
metamorphosis. Where a chasm exists between spirit and matter
for contemporary thinking, Steiner has a spectrum of intermedi-
ate stages which provide a framework for understanding how
God incarnated in Jesus, in what sense the miracles were
possible, how Christ's death and especially how the Resurrection of his physical body could occur.

Steiner's detailed account of the origin of the universe offers

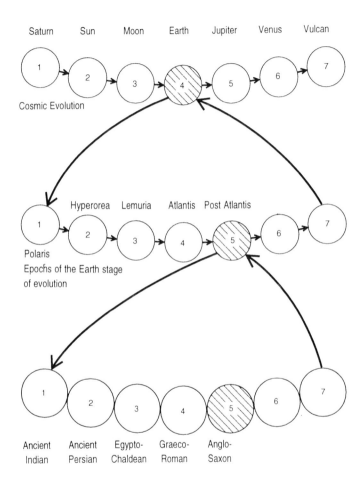

Steiner's cosmology relative to the present time.

a new approach to the problem of the relationship between spirit and matter; however, like traditional theology, it also presupposes the existence of spiritual beings. In his book *Occult Science: an Outline,* Steiner gives a full description of how the earth has come to its present state. Using traditional terms, he describes how the hierarchies of angelic beings worked through three separate stages or 'incarnations' of the earth in order to create the world as we experience it today. These stages were necessary to create the earth and humanity in all their complexity.

The first three stages, called Saturn, Sun and Moon, are followed by our present earth existence, which in turn will be followed by three additional developmental stages called Jupiter (known in the Bible as the New Jerusalem), Venus and Vulcan. In each of these stages we will have an opportunity to evolve into higher spiritual forms. Earth itself unfolds in seven stages, each of which consists of seven subdivisions, as indicated in the chart opposite showing Steiner's cosmology relative to the present time.

Like Dionysus the Areopagite, Rudolf Steiner describes in detail nine hierarchies of spiritual beings working over vast expanses of space and time to create the universe in which we live. However, Steiner's description of these hierarchies, their origins, intentions and modes of working, is very different from the Areopagite's whose hierarchies merely represent increasing degrees of goodness and light. Steiner's description is much more differentiated. However for reasons of space it must suffice here to list their names: the first hierarchy, closest to us consists of angels, archangels and the archai; the second consists of Exousiai, Dynameis, Kyriotetes; the third consists of the Thrones, Cherubim and Seraphim. We are located, in terms of spiritual evolution, one step below the angels, while the animals, plants and minerals represent the three stages below the human.

Because of Steiner's detailed descriptions of the activities of angelic beings, he has sometimes been unjustly accused of polytheism. However, for Steiner, God is one, although he distinguishes the three aspects of the Father, the Son and the

First hierarchy	Seraphim *or* Spirits of Love
	Cherubim *or* Spirits of Harmony
	Thrones *or* Spirits of Will
Second hierarchy	Kyriotetes *or* Spirits of Wisdom *also called* Dominions
	Dynameis *or* Spirits of Movement *also called* Mights *or* Virtues
	Exousiai *or* Spirits of Form *also called* Powers
Third hierarchy	Archai *or* Spirits of Personality *also called* Principalities
	Archangels *or* Folk Spirits *also called* Fire Spirits
	Angels *or* Messengers *also called* Sons of Life *or* of Twilight
The human being	

The angelic hierarchies

Holy Spirit. To understand how the many angelic beings of the hierarchies are related to the one God, we can think of how the human I, the self, is related to the body. In one sense the self stands *above* and rules the body with all its limbs. But the I also lives within the body and permeates the limbs. The body with its individual parts is not the human being but serves to reveal him. Similarly God uses the orders of the Angels as body and limbs to create and maintain the world in the same way that we make use of our arms and hands to work on earth.

Mosaic in the roof of the Baptistry in Florence showing the nine hierarchies of angels with their Latin names.

Evil

It is impossible to describe the development of humankind without an understanding of the adversary powers. The riddle of evil, however, is such that no answer, no matter how *intellectually* satisfying, can ever satisfy our hearts. Because we are rational creatures our attempts to come to terms with the riddle

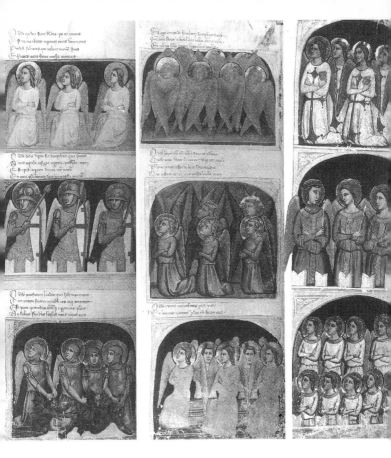

The nine hierarchies of angels from a fourteenth-century Italian adddress in Latin verse by Robert of Anjou.

of why God allows injustice, pain and suffering must always begin with thinking. But our humanity, which is based on even deeper levels of existence, will constantly re-ask the question: 'Why must it be?' The ongoing and continually renewed effort to answer this question deepens and expands our consciousness of what it means to be human, of what the struggle between good and evil actually means. We grow and evolve spiritually by continually having to ask and try to answer this question.

Steiner sees all beings, including the angelic, in a process of evolving. In the distant past there were beings that rebelled and renounced the possibility of progressing upward in their own evolution. Their renunciation was, in a sense, a sacrifice necessary for us to develop free will. Through this rebellion they became, during earth evolution, what we experience as evil. Living within the spiritual atmosphere of the earth itself, they can influence us directly, especially in our feelings and our will impulses, realms in which we are not fully conscious. For Steiner, then, evil is a reality represented by real beings. It is *not* the mere absence of the Good.

The story in Genesis of the serpent in the garden indicates that evil did not begin with Adam and Eve. Lacking knowledge of good and evil, Eve could not have known that it was evil to disobey God and eat the fruit of the tree of knowledge of good and evil. Yet Adam and Eve and their offspring must bear the consequences: children must be born in pain and human beings must work on the earth in order to eat. Eventually, all must die. But this curse from God is, like any 'curse' from God, a blessing in disguise. We see in these archetypal images the path we must tread to overcome death and once again return to heaven. In the image of child-bearing we see that the purpose of pain is to bring forth new life, while the work of tilling the soil is a picture for the purpose of all work: the transformation of the earth including the human beings who live upon it.

Only abstractly can we speak of the opposition of good and evil. In specific life-situations, good is not simply opposed to evil. We are not presented with a simple choice. In concrete earthly situations, evil is split within itself and forms a duality. For example, bravery and cowardice are not opposites. The virtue of bravery is actually found between two evils: recklessness and cowardice. Every virtue is located between two kinds of evil. According to Steiner there are two fallen beings, Lucifer and Ahriman, who unceasingly seek to pull us away from the centre.

Lucifer appeals to our pride and ambition. He wants us to think we have no limitations. The story of the tower of Babel and the Greek story of Icarus who flew too close to the sun are

Adam
and Eve.
*Fresco
in the
Bran-
cacci
Chapel,
Florence,
by Ma-
saccio.*

Luciferic	Virtue	Ahrimanic
underestimation of the earthly		*overestimation of the earthly*
wastefulness	thriftiness	miserliness
arrogance	self-confidence	lack of self-confidence
disorderliness	orderliness	pedantry
recklessness	bravery	cowardice
vacillation	equanimity	rigidity
over-susceptibility	interest	apathy
ruthless ambition	perseverance	indolence
effusiveness	compassion	coldness

The good is not just a point of balance between two evil extremes. It is a higher unity within which one-sided forces serve something better. The two forces leading to evil find a form of redemption in the good achieved by human beings.

two examples of his influence. In Lucifer's eyes humanity should retain the natural powers of clairvoyance possessed by everyone in earlier times. We should cling to the old religious forms that appeal mainly to emotions; the spiritual revelations and old philosophies like those of ancient India are still the best even for today. While threatening our progress in this way Lucifer does aid us in another. His divine sense of self-esteem, of self-worth and pride inspired Eve in the Garden thereby setting into motion the flow of human spiritual evolution. Ultimately it can lead us to freedom. Lucifer is also responsible for our love of beauty and art for they both touch on the divine.

Lucifer (left). Detail from Rudolf Steiner's Group sculpture.
Ahriman (right). Study for the Group sculpture.

They allow us to sense the grandeur of the spiritual world. Nevertheless, he does not want us to be fully conscious or to be truly independent of him.

Ahriman's realm is the material earth and he is infinitely clever. Because he knows all about the physical forces within the earth he constantly 'inspires' us to make new discoveries and invent new machines. Ahriman seeks the opposite of Lucifer. Where Lucifer would hold us back, Ahriman wishes us to advance far faster than is good for us. He wants us to have earthly experiences and to employ earthly forces long before our I has developed the moral forces necessary for proper use of those forces. For him 'the future is already here.' By fore-shortening our development he hopes to prevent us from reaching our goal of freedom. He loves a razor-sharp intellect that has been narrowed and specialized until it understands one aspect of the world to the exclusion of all others. Such specialization gives power and Ahriman revels in earthly power.

In sum, Luciferic beings lead us to *underestimate* and flee from the earth while Ahrimanic beings lead us to *overestimate* and crave the earth. The human I finds itself in freedom through struggling against their power. Overestimation of the earth is followed by hardening, cramp, estrangement from the spiritual, stagnation, paralysis and death. Underestimation of the earth is accompanied by intoxication, disintegration, loss of form, illusion, and insanity.

We can see the interplay between these two forms of evil in every field. In religion, too much 'other worldliness,' nebulous mysticism and rejection of the earthly reality of human existence is the work of Lucifer. The influence of Ahriman is revealed in the cold, abstract, earth-bound logic that denies reality to any but those aspects of earth existence which can be grasped, weighed, measured and, whenever possible, brought under the rigid laws of mathematics. This polarity is seen also in two extreme views of Jesus Christ. One, a variation on an ancient Gnostic error, sees Christ as a mythological being, not as a historical personality. This being need not even have incarnated in an earthly body to have founded Christianity. The other view sees Jesus as a simple man who lived a very moral life not unlike Socrates; the inspiration of his death was alone sufficient to begin a new religion, for obviously the Resurrection could not have been a real event.

According to Steiner we actually need both Lucifer and Ahriman. When kept in their place they help us to attain our goals on earth. We need the pride and self esteem which come from Lucifer to remind us that we are spiritual beings who have ideals and that at times we should reach for the stars regardless of our earthly situation. So, too, we need a sober estimation of our possibilities based on the weight of our earthly situation. But we must never become arrogant with the thought that we actually belong to a higher world nor contemptuous of ideals from a higher world carried in the human heart. We see here

how these two tempters, called Satan (Ahriman) and the Devil
(Lucifer) in the Bible, reach into our very experience of self,
that is, into the place where our I lives. This is very serious, for
the whole purpose of human history and evolution is found in
the I.

Early evolution

After descending into matter and awakening to himself as an I,
the human being begins to experience, eventually to understand
and control, his physical environment. Life on the earth with its
work and suffering enables him then to extend his I through the
transformation of his physical, etheric and astral bodies into
eternal, spiritual substance. This transformation takes place as
the I becomes master or 'Lord' over his thinking, feeling and
will. The adversary powers contend with us as to who will gain
mastery over these parts, or our soul.

   In order to understand the nature of evil and the meaning of
the Jesus Christ's appearance, it is necessary to give Steiner's
account of how the human being has evolved over the ages.
Vast ages of time were involved in the descent of the human I
into matter and the evolved human bodies. Long, long ago
certain Luciferic beings interfered with our development. Under
their influence we sought a measure of independence from the
guidance of higher beings before the time originally set for such
freedom to be granted. As a result, the human I became too
deeply infused with the material environment. The time before
Lucifer's intervention is referred to in the Bible as paradise. It
can be said that the I became too quickly self-conscious. As a
result, humanity became selfish and greedy. Since then we have
been prey to the illusion that by increasing our earthly, material
possessions we can increase our true selves. Actually, our true
I, our higher self can really only increase itself by transforming
earthly experience and matter into spiritual wisdom and spiritual
substance.

   The Luciferic interference ultimately influenced the forces
within the earth itself and brought about a series of great vol-

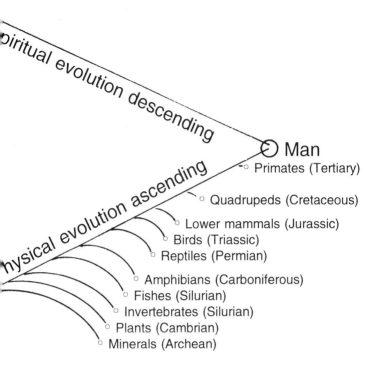

The evolution of man and animals (after Poppelbaum)

canic catastrophes. Although this age saw all the kingdoms of nature becoming harder and denser, the process had not yet advanced to the point where the physical forms of living beings were fixed. Hence, there are no traces left today of the life forms of that time.

At this point one aspect of human physical evolution should be mentioned. The fossil record is not contested by Steiner but his view of earth's past gives an interpretation entirely different from Darwin's. According to anthroposophy, the animals actually evolved from the human being but from a time before he had become a physical, visible being. Animals are beings that descended from the spiritual world and incarnated 'prematurely,' becoming hardened and fixed in form before the human organism had developed to the stage where it could bear an individual spirit and soul. They descended from the archetype of the human being and took on bodies that were physical counterparts of their astral bodies at that time. Without individual I's they could not evolve further. Each member of the animal kingdom is derived from, and corresponds to some part of the human being.[10] The primates incarnated last before us, having evolved up to the stage where they had bodies similar to those of human beings.

The next stage of human evolution is called by Steiner the Atlantean in keeping with ancient esoteric tradition. The earth during the first part of that age was still so soft and malleable that there are no physical traces remaining. During this time Man's inner life developed as the human I began to express itself in the etheric body. We did not yet have any ability to reason but were guided by an almost continuous memory.

Eventually Atlantis was destroyed by a violent catastrophe of storm and flood caused by human moral depravity. This is the same event described in the Bible as the Flood. The survivors migrated eastwards to Africa, Europe and Asia. The greatest leader of these migrations is referred to in the Bible as Noah.

After the Flood the human physical body was no longer in a mobile, malleable form. It had hardened into a fixed, solid form that therefore could provide the basis for rational thought to develop. Thus begins the gradual unfolding of the capacity for rational thought. There follow seven post-Atlantean 'cultural epochs' each lasting approximately 2160 years. Each of these epochs marks a pronounced change in human consciousness. Around 7200 BC the first, the 'old Indian,' began. Echoes of this ancient civilization can be found in the earliest Vedas, first written down much later when direct clairvoyance was dying out. Until the demise of natural clairvoyance these sublime teachings had been preserved as a kind of folk memory. There had been no reason to write them down.

When imagining what the conditions of life were like for these ancient peoples we cannot overstress how unlike us they

Noah and the Flood from the Bedford Book of Hours.

Ahura Mazdao. Relief from Khorsabad, now in the Louvre.

were. They could still perceive the spiritual world and spiritual beings while the physical world was experienced as only vaguely real. Higher spiritual beings were worshipped as gods and spoke through the leaders of these ancient civilizations. Elemental beings helped people with their day to day business.

The spirits ensouling springs, rivers, holy trees and some mountains were experienced by the human beings alive at this time.[11] Every different people had different names for these nature spirits. In northern Europe they were called trolls, kobolds, elves, gnomes, salamanders or fire spirits, sylphs, undines, and so on. They all belonged to the reality of daily life in ancient cultures. Certain rituals and ceremonies ensured their friendly cooperation. The myths and legends of the ancients are echoes of memories left in the place of actual perceptions. Fairy tales and legends are the last remnants of those echoes. There was no I consciousness, no self-awareness, no possibility of freedom. The adversary powers could do little in old India because the astral body, the seat of passions and desires, was not yet developed.

In the first epoch people felt that earth was Maya, an illusion, and that their real life was as spiritual beings in a world of spirit. In the second, the Persian epoch (about 5100 BC to 2900 BC) they were taught to regard the earth as their true home. Natural clairvoyance began to fail in large segments of the population. The darkness of the earth was beckoning. The great teacher of this age was called Zarathustra (or Zoroaster) who taught that the physical world is not mere lifeless matter for human use or enjoyment. Behind the physical earth is a world of spirit. Zarathustra's mission was to reveal the nature of the great Sun Spirit, Ahura Mazdao, the god of light, and to expose the work of the evil god, Ahriman, the lord of darkness. He taught that Ahura Mazdao, the Sun spirit will one day descend to the earth and defeat Ahriman. In one form or another this teaching has appeared in all subsequent religions.

In the third post-Atlantean epoch, beginning in the third millennium BC, the Sumerian, Assyrian, Babylonian, Egyptian civilizations reigned. As the human being began to have an inner consciousness of his soul life, he began to develop and transform his astral body. The guidance of human feeling required for this development was accomplished by religion. Spiritual and political guidance, which were completely undifferentiated at the beginning of this age, came through the great initiates and priest kings, who were themselves inspired and guided by higher beings. In the earliest part of this epoch the priest-kings were invariably guided by higher spiritual beings. As the next age approached, leaders came to increasingly experience themselves not only as servants of higher beings but also as earthly individuals wielding power. This led, of course, to the first appearances of political and religious corruption.

The intellectual thinking so widespread among Greeks was not yet possible. The physical phenomena of earth did not yet require rational explanation. Egyptian mythology, for example, contained many different myths explaining creation. Not only did these stories contain internal contradictions; they were also often in logical conflict with one another. But only rational thinking would notice this. It did not trouble the Egyptians. Contradiction belongs to thinking and not to feelings.

Yahweh, the Hebrews and the Law

Polytheism was natural for the peoples living in the first three post-Atlantean epochs. Human beings could still sense, if not actually perceive, the spiritual beings behind all nature. As this participation was gradually dying out, the power to think abstractly emerged with the Hebrews, the originators of monotheism. The development of monotheism was also gradual. Yahweh first told Abraham and the other patriarchs that they must worship him alone. It was centuries before Moses and then all the prophets taught that theirs was the only God. Like children who were always forgetting and disobeying, the Hebrews were constantly 'backsliding' and worshipping other gods, especially the fertility gods who promised them sons.

According to Steiner, Yahweh, the god of the Hebrews, was a being related to Christ in exactly the same way moon light is related to sun light. The light of Christ was guiding the Hebrews but only after it had been reflected off the moon, so to speak. Christ, the Son God himself was working throught this reflected spiritual light, in one of his pre-earthly forms, to prepare humanity for the coming of the self-conscious I. As the configuration of the human soul changed, monotheism became

Elijah fed by the Raven *by Giovanni Savoldo.*

possible and with it a personal relationship to God. Such an individual relationship to God is necessary for the human I to experience itself as an I, as a self. Elijah's experience, for example, described in 1 Kings 19 — that God was not to be found in the earthquake, whirlwind or fire but was present as a still quiet voice within — marked an essential step on this path to the self-conscious experience of the I. Gradually this experience has become the basic constituent of human consciousness. We have become aware of ourselves as selves.

Moses breaking the Tablets of the Law *by Rembrandt.*

The task of the Hebrews was to make the full incarnation of the human I possible. As Steiner explained, Isaiah's prophecy concerning 'the Lord' to come (Isaiah 40:3–5) actually referred to the I in the human soul:

> We have in the soul, when we look to the astral body, various forces. We usually call them thinking, feeling, and the will. The soul thinks, feels, and wills. Those are the three forces that work in the soul. But they are the serving forces of the soul. As Man progressed in evolution, these forces which formerly were themselves the lords ... became subject to the Kyrios, the Lord of the soul forces, the I. Nothing else was understood by this word, *Kyrios,* when it referred to the soul, than the I. It was no longer true that the divine spiritual thinks, feels, wills in me, but *I* think, *I* feel, *I* will: The Lord became a presence to be reckoned with among the other forces in the soul. Prepare yourselves, you human souls, to follow the Kyrios, the Lord, in your souls: 'Listen, to the call in the loneliness of the soul: Prepare the force or the direction of the lord of the soul, of the I. Open to his forces!' This is the meaning any translation must capture: 'Open to the I's forces, so that the Lord of the soul can come in, so that it is not the slave of thinking, feeling, and willing.' And if you translate these words: 'Behold, that which is "I-ness," "egohood" itself, sends its angel before you, who should give you the possibility to understand how the I calls in the loneliness of the astral soul: prepare the directions of the I, open, the soul forces for the I ...' — then you have meaning in these significant words of the prophet Isaiah; then you have reference to the greatest event in human evolution; thus you understand how he points out that human loneliness of soul longs for the arrival of the Lord in the soul, of the I. Then the words get force and weight. Thus must we grasp such words.[12]

The higher self of the human being, necessary for true freedom,

could enter humanity only with Christ's entry into Jesus of
Nazareth. The preparation of a human body capable of receiv-
ing this higher being was a part of the Hebrew mission. As the
'I am' of humanity gradually approached earth, he created the
nation of the Hebrews from his dwelling place in the spiritual
spheres above earth. In a discussion of Moses' conversation
with Yahweh on Mount Sinai, Steiner says:

> Thus was proclaimed what was later to enter the world
> through Christ Jesus. We hear the name of the Logos,
> we hear him at that time calling to Moses, 'I am the I
> AM!' The Logos proclaims his name, that part of himself
> which can be comprehended through the understanding,
> through the intellect. What is here proclaimed appears in
> the flesh as the Logos, is incarnated in Christ Jesus.'[13]

The Mosaic law was given to show how the true human I
would behave in the moral sphere when it was incarnated.
Individual human beings were not yet capable of evolving these
principles out of their own inner being. The law also enhanced
human thinking through the exacting concentration required to
observe it. This brought about a turning inward and away from
any experience of the divine in the surrounding world. Although
the Jews learned to admire nature as the work of God, God
himself was not experienced as immanent *within* nature.

The Christian path into the future

Another people also gradually developed the ability to experience the divine within, but through entirely different means.
During the fourth post Atlantean epoch which began with the
Greek and Roman civilizations and extended to approximately
1400 AD, humanity completed its descent from spiritual worlds.
Fully incarnated on earth, humanity could now, through the
conscious activity of the human I, begin its ascent again into
spiritual worlds. This ascent is not to be thought of as a retreat
from earthly consciousness but rather as based upon such con-

sciousness. The earth and its forms must not be left behind.
According to Steiner the ascent is only possible because God
incarnated in Jesus of Nazareth. He experienced human selfhood, died as a human being and was resurrected as a human
being become a god. Furthermore, Christ Jesus is now united
for all eternity with the destiny of humanity. Because our
conscious, earthly I is the place-holder in the human soul for
our true I's which are borne in Christ, we can experience Christ
consciously in our inmost selves.

Humanity has a long path to tread in order to understand the
meaning of Christ's coming; during the Greek and Roman
epoch humankind took a decisive step on that path. It began to
learn how to *understand* the world with the aid of thinking, at
first the world of earth and then, with time, the world of spirit.

In the present epoch we have entered the physical world to
such an extent that we tend to experience only ourselves as
subjects and others as objects. This is a necessary stage but we
must pass through it to once again experience the divine in the
other. This excessive consciousness of self as subject, that is,
our I-consciousness, is nearly entirely based on experiencing
our environment through the physical body. But nothing in the
physical world can tell us who we are, what we should do or
explain the meaning of life. The cultural manifestations of this
loss of meaning is found in some of the post-modern movements. Imprisoned in our physical bodies, we find it increasingly difficult to reach out with our souls to 'the other.' In
these philosophies the engine of logical connection is still run-
ning but our spiritual and psychological moorings are lost. As
a result, elaborate and fantastical theories are created. Although
absurd they are difficult to ignore because of their logical
consistency, even when they argue against any reason inherent
in the universe. It is nearly impossible for modern consciousness to imagine how God could actually intervene in the world.
Gone are the ancient hierarchical structures of being, with God
and the angels above and the human being below and the devil
even lower. Gone is any framework affording a spiritual orien-
tation. In its place is a religion reduced to an interpretation of
texts, 'God is dead' theologies, and social work. Much of

humanity today stands before an empty grave. The Old and New Testaments are usually interpreted in our times entirely from the point of view of their socio-cultural contexts. There is no need to consider divine intervention. *There is no need to assume the existence of a spiritual world above and behind the physical world and the world of human souls.*

Before the modern age the human beings could discern intimations of spirit in the unfolding of human thinking and logic; in the modern age thinking and logic no longer automatically give us an experience of spirit and now, in the culture of post-modernism, human thinking and logic are considered a sham and deserve our suspicion. This is the age we now live in. The descent into matter necessary to bring the human I to full consciousness has created the apparently unbridgeable duality of matter and spirit, reason and faith. The solution to the dichotomy lies in the human I. In a verse from 1918 Steiner says:

Through the wide world there lives and moves
The essence of the human being,
While in the innermost core of the human being
The mirror-image of the World is living.

The I unites the two,
And thus creates
The Meaning of existence.[14]

The bridge between ourselves and others can only be reached by the path to the spirit within us, through the arrival of the Lord in the soul, through the awareness of 'Christ within us.'

The bridge between us and nature can only be reached on this path. But the Christian relationship to nature has two extremes to avoid: the Luciferic and Ahrimanic. Modern civilization is based on the Ahrimanic: the notion that nature is filled with spiritless, dead matter having nothing to do with God. Regarding nature and matter in this way has led humanity to misinterpret God's words recorded in Genesis 1:28: 'Be fruitful and multiply and fill the earth and subdue *[or* dominate] it.'

Only recently, after centuries of Ahrimanic exploitation, have we come to realize that our mastery of nature also implies a *responsibility to care for and nurture* that part of the universe that is below us.

Now we see in some quarters how revulsion for the damage done to nature by unthinking, arrogant men and women has lead some people into the hands of Lucifer. He would have us confuse the beauty and goodness of nature with the beauty and goodness of divine being itself. The danger is that we forget the transitory, evolving aspect of nature. Those who esteem nature above humanity are ultimately valuing unconsciousness above consciousness and forgetting that death and destruction is the rule in nature as much as in humanity.

A Christian path between these two extremes must be found. In Genesis 3:28 we read that the ground is cursed because of the deed of Adam and Eve. And in Chapter 8 of Romans Paul speaks of creation being 'in bondage to decay' because of human will. We must remember that the goodness in nature comes from God while the temporal aspect is our doing. Creation, nature itself, will be saved from the effects of the Fall only through the conscious, human I that accepts responsibility for nature's condition and works to bring salvation to it. By transforming it and lifting it up to the spirit in our consciousness we must learn how to release the spiritual beings 'enchanted' in matter.

3. God and Christ Jesus

The Trinity

Rudolf Steiner's vision into spiritual worlds presented him with a highly differentiated panorama of spiritual beings. For this reason he was often accused of being a polytheist, one who believes in many gods. But what is a 'god'? If we mean a being higher than Man then, according to old Christian traditions, there are nine levels of angelic beings above humanity. According to Steiner, the divine being to whom people pray at any given time is not always easy to determine. When human beings feel or speak of 'God,' they may actually be referring to any number of different higher beings.

Throughout history many different spiritual beings have inspired and guided the evolution of humankind. So we see the word 'God' used throughout the ages to describe different experiences of the divine. What unites all these experiences is the Godhead itself shining through the various beings. This is made possible through the principle of indwelling whereby the higher spiritual beings manifest and work through the lower. Standing above and shining through the nine hierarchies of angels is the Trinity, the Godhead in its threefold nature: the Father, the Son and the Holy Spirit. God thought of as the highest being above all 'indwells' in various ways all lower beings.

On many occasions and from different points of view Steiner has described the Trinity. In a lecture Steiner said:

The Trinity. Detail from the Disputa *by Raphael.*

The Father is the unbegotten begetter who places the Son into the physical world. But at the same time the Father uses the Holy Spirit in order to tell humanity that in the spirit, the supersensory is comprehensible, ... And when Christ sent the Holy Spirit to his disciples — this imparting occurred through the Christ, through the Son. For this reason it was an ancient dogma that the Father is the unbegotten begetter, that the Son is the one begotten by the Father, and that the Holy Spirit is the one imparted to humanity by the Father and the Son. This is not some kind of arbitrarily asserted dogma but rather the wisdom of initiation living in the earliest Christian centuries; only later was it covered over and buried along with the teachings concerning the Trichotomy and the Trinity.

The divine principle working as Christianity within evolving humanity cannot be understood without the Trinity. If, in the place of the Trinity, some other teaching concerning God were to enter, then, basically speaking, it would not be a fully Christian teaching. One must understand the Father, the Son, and the Holy Spirit if one would understand the teaching concerning God concretely and in a genuine way.[15]

For Steiner it is absolutely essential to understand that God is actively present in the universe in three different ways. Without such an understanding, Christianity and its claims are inexplicable.

• The Father God as the ground of existence is the one behind all being. He is above all space and outside time, without beginning and without end, absolutely perfect being. Physical space is the dead shadow of the Father God.

However, if God were *only* the ground of existence, the solid granite upon which reality rests, then the universe would be dead, rigid, lifeless. But he is not the victim of his own perfection. He is also the God, who is constantly becoming and growing forth into the future. God the Son stands behind all life, all creation, all transformation and evolution. As stated at the beginning of John's Gospel, the Son is the creator of the world. Since all becoming presupposes it, time is the living picture of the Son God. In his incarnation in time, in history as Christ Jesus, human and divine history are united. He became the Son of Man, the quintessence of the highest stage of development to which the human being may aspire. Because both divine and human futures coincide in him he is called both the Son of God and the Son of Man. God has entered nature, his original revelation, the existing world of the Father. God has created a new place to 'grow,' to express the divine in a way never seen before. Humankind is God's 'frontier.'

The Holy Spirit is God as pure spirit, as the highest wisdom, as a knowing conscious being. Although these characteristics and functions can also be attributed to both the other persons of the Trinity, they can nevertheless be distinguished as the expression of an 'independent' being. We can develop a sense for the Father by thinking of the foundation of our being; we can sense the Son by feeling the surging rhythms of life's energy; but we are aware of the Spirit within us directly through the fact of our consciousness. Although a world of ideas can live in our minds without our being in God, the *possibility* of such a mental life is given to us by the Spirit God.

The Fall and human thinking

It is only due to the Fall that our consciousness has also become fallen, capable of combining thoughts in ways that are not true. However, as we have seen in Chapter 1, duality of self versus world, the very creation of the 'other' and of our experience of alienation is the result of the activity of the fallen self. Through thinking our consciousness splits the world into object and subject. Some spiritual movements would seek to overcome this existential alienation by simply denying the significance of rational thinking. They seem to favour a return to a pre-rational state of mind when the contents of consciousness were not yet differentiated. Such a pre-rational state is imagined to be closer to creation, that is, nature and hence, the creator. Harmony and goodness are sought through a return to a state before the Fall.

Such tendencies are seen in the 'creation spirituality' of Matthew Fox who seeks, in his words, 'to overcome the stale categories of fall/redemption theology.'[16] But for Rudolf Steiner the Fall is not a mere category that we arbitrarily choose. Both the Fall and its consequences are historical facts with profound consequences for human consciousness. In a lecture Steiner said:

> We must go back to ... the event which is indicated for us in the Old Testament as the temptation through the serpent. This event is of a very remarkable kind. From its outcome all men suffer as long as they are subject to incarnation. ... Through this event ... they become more closely entangled in matter, allegorically designated as the 'Fall of Man.' But it was the fall that first called Man to his present individuality. ... Through this event man has indeed attained to the power of love and to freedom.[17]

According to Steiner then, without the consequences of the Fall, an event both mythical *and* historical, love and freedom are impossible. New Age philosophies and spiritual movements that would deny the historical reality of the Fall would also forgo true freedom, love and ultimately, individuality. Since the Fall our relationship to the spirit has changed. It became possible for us to know the world and ourselves. This knowing is flawed but contains the seeds of our possible redemption. The path forward must be *through* thinking and into the spiritual world, not a *retreat* from thinking *back* into the spiritual world. Although our thinking may presently be fallen, we can nevertheless attain to truth and understanding of the world through a thinking that has been 'purified' or 'healed.' This can happen when our efforts are met by the grace of the Holy Spirit.[18] The healing of the world begins within our human thinking when the Spirit God enters our consciousness and gives us insights into reality. We thereby unite the world of earth with the world of spirit. Steiner's understanding reminds us very much of German idealism. God's creature, the human being, recognizes himself in his divine mission: the Divine becoming conscious in Nature: God as Holy Spirit.

The truth of the Trinity was not taught for the first time in Christianity. There were many pre-Christian mythologies and religions that also recognized a Trinity of some kind. But the great difference for Christianity is this: that the second person of the Trinity has moved into a special relationship to humanity. Through the Son God, humankind has been given a new path to the Father and the Spirit. In a sense, the Son God summarizes the entire Trinity within himself. The static elements of the Father and the Holy Spirit, eternal being and wisdom, surge into the dynamic world of earth through the consciousness of the Son, who has united heaven and earth. This union was brought about through the already mentioned principle of 'indwelling,' whereby a lower being makes a sacrifice in order to become a vehicle for a higher being.

Blood ties and Christ

Pre-Christian religions reflected Christ's activity as he descended through the spiritual world into earthly incarnation. Every ethnic group was guided by spiritual beings. Although individuals comprising these groups experienced the divine primarily in the world around them in ancient times, they also experienced it directly within themselves through the blood which gave them an unshakable sense of ethnic belonging as well as their sense of self. Through their ancestors, who were often seen as gods or as inspired by gods, they knew who they themselves were and what their relationship to God was. According to Steiner, this way of relating to the divine through the blood was to change with the advent of Christ. In his lectures on John's Gospel Steiner explains in great detail how John expressed Christ's essence as the 'I am,' distinguishing it from the consciousness of self existing before.

The followers of the Old Testament ... would have said: 'My consciousness reaches up to the father of the whole

people, to Abraham; we — I and the father Abraham —
are one. A common ego encompasses us all, and I only
feel myself safe within the whole folk-substance.' Thus
the followers of the Old Testament looked up to father
Abraham and said: 'I and father Abraham are one! In
my veins flows the same blood that flows in the veins of
Abraham.' They felt father Abraham as the root from
which every individual Abrahamite had sprung as a stem.

The Christ-Jesus came and said to his nearest, most
intimate initiates: Hitherto, mankind has judged only
according to the flesh, according to blood-relationship,
men have been conscious of reposing within a higher
invisible union. But you should believe in a still higher
spiritual relationship, in one that reaches beyond the
blood-tie. You should believe in a spiritual Father-sub-
stance in which the I is rooted, and which is more spiritual than the substance which as a group-soul binds the
Jewish people together. You should believe in what
reposes within me and within every human being, in
what is not only one with Abraham, but one with the
very divine foundation of the world. Therefore, Christ-
Jesus, according to the Gospel of St John, emphasizes
the words: 'Before Father Abraham was, was the I AM!'
My primal ego mounts not only to the Father-Principle
that reaches back to Abraham, but my I is one with all
that pulses through the entire cosmos, and to this my
spiritual nature soars aloft. I and the Father are one!
These are important words which one should experience;
then will one feel the forward bound made by mankind,
a bound which advanced human evolution further in
consequence of that impulse given by the advent of the
Christ. The Christ was the mighty quickener of the
'I AM.'[19]

This conception of Christ has consequences for evaluating
the revival of old ethnic groups so often seen today. Because it
is difficult to find an experience of community today, many
people are tempted to reach back into the blood ties. The search

for solid ground in the soul has led many to limit their sense of self to a community based on the physical and accidental circumstances of their birth. This emphasis on ethnic communities has sometimes reached the point where the desire for individual expression is even considered a threat to community life. Instead of asking what they can do for humanity, individuals who might otherwise strive to say with Christ, 'I and the Father are one,' are encouraged to explore, nurture and defend their own blood community and its rights over and against other groups. In Steiner's Christology all human beings are brothers and sisters. Any family smaller than humanity is pre-Christian at best. This is not to say that individuals in any family or ethnic group cannot be Christians. Indeed, family life with its constant need for sacrifice provides one of the best environments for learning to be a Christian. However, membership in any group defined by blood ties says nothing about the intrinsic goodness or Christianity of its members.

Baptism and temptation

Returning to the question of who Christ Jesus was, we see a great descent from the highest God imaginable down to the human level: the Father God sent his Son who 'restrained' the radiant power of his being in sacrifice after sacrifice, in order to gradually descend to the human level. When Jesus of Nazareth was baptized in the River Jordan, the Son of God, the Logos, the Creator, entered into that place in the soul of Jesus where the I of a human being lives. Stepping forth from the River Jordan, Christ, the creator of heaven and earth, saw through the eyes of a human being what had become of the earth and humanity. He experienced his creation, as it were, from the 'outside,' the side that had been crystallized out of the spiritual world. In the etheric body of Jesus he found the memories of the wisest man ever to walk on the earth, the wisdom of Zarathustra. In the astral body he found the noblest and purest feeling of anyone who had ever walked on earth, the compassion of Buddha. He walked in a physical body which

had been prepared through forty-two generations from Abraham to Jesus. Only such a body could receive into itself the power of this divine being, a power that would have shattered any ordinary body.

Immediately after the Baptism, Christ was led or 'driven' by the Spirit into the wilderness where he was tempted by the devil. According to Steiner this temptation came from the two beings already mentioned, Lucifer and Ahriman.

Ahriman, the adversary who wants us to recognize the material world alone, suggested that he transform stones into bread with a mere command. Christ could have done this. He could have provided humanity with the bread of life at any time, but would thereby have robbed us of part of our path to salvation. It is our task to work on the earth, to transform the earth through work into a form that can nourish us. In this work we must learn to use all Ahriman's gifts without succumbing to him. We would never have a chance to become free beings if we had received the bread of life at once and never learned to transform Ahrimanic 'bread' into heavenly Bread. When Christ responded to this temptation by saying that 'man shall not live by bread alone, but by every word of God' (Luke 4:4) he is telling us that the material world is necessary but not sufficient for our evolution.

Lucifer, the adversary who wishes us to flee the earth before our I develops into its fullness, also tempted Christ. If Christ had yielded to his temptation to become a political leader with all the glory of this world, then humankind may well have followed Christ, but we would never have become free. Neither did Christ after the Resurrection choose to show himself to the Romans who had crucified him. He revealed himself only to those, who out of the innermost divine power in their hearts had struggled in freedom to recognize him as the redeemer.

When both Lucifer and Ahriman took him to the pinnacle of the temple he was confronted with a twofold temptation. Because the temple was in the heart of Jerusalem, casting himself down from the pinnacle would have been witnessed by

The Baptism *by Piero della Francesca.*

thousands. Such a magical act would have bedazzled the masses
and they would have followed him for the wrong reasons; again
they would have been left unfree.

The healings and the transformation of Jesus

Christ's respect for our freedom is seen also in his actions after
performing miracles. He usually instructed those he had healed
not to tell anyone. Furthermore, he only allowed his healing
forces to work when the I of the person needing healing was
active. Hence, the question recorded in the Gospels, 'Do you
want to be healed?' The initiative for healing came from the
sick themselves, not from Christ. He did not want people to
believe in him because he healed. At that time in history there
were many who could heal and even some prepared to use
supersensory faculties to influence the course of history.[20] It is
also significant that most of the healings recorded in the
Gospels occurred at the *beginning* of his ministry when Christ's
divine power was so great that, in a sense, it simply overflowed
to those in need of healing whose faith allowed it. With the
passage of time those forces were consumed in the transformation of Jesus and the ongoing encounter with death.

Immediately after the Baptism, the I of Christ began to work
in the soul of Jesus. In a series of scenes from the gospels we
see the effects of this penetration and transformation of Jesus'
astral, etheric and physical bodies. The waves that Jesus walked
on before the sight of his disciples were upon the sea of life
forces. This vision showed the disciples the soul freed from the
excessive influence of the life forces which have an ethereal,
watery quality. So too the feeding of thousands was a reflection, on the earthly level of images, of the nourishment which
streamed from a purified and transformed astral body filled with
compassion for humanity. Through the I of Christ the soul of
Jesus became bread, became free of the sickness of original sin,
that is free of the excessive influence from the lower self.

As the Christ penetrated down into the life forces of Jesus
of Nazareth the life body of Jesus became free and paradisal

again. Because his etheric body no longer needed light from the soul and spirit it began to shine forth by itself. The achievement of this stage of penetration and transformation is recorded in Chapter 17 of Matthew's gospel in the story of the transfiguration when, upon Mount Tabor, 'his face shone like the sun, and his garments became white as light.'

In Steiner's lectures on the Gospels he describes how the physical body was permeated when Christ rode into Jerusalem on Palm Sunday. The substance of Jesus' body had been plumbed to the depths by the spirit of Christ whose presence had healed the restless craving nature of material substance and transformed it into a selfless state hitherto unseen in the world

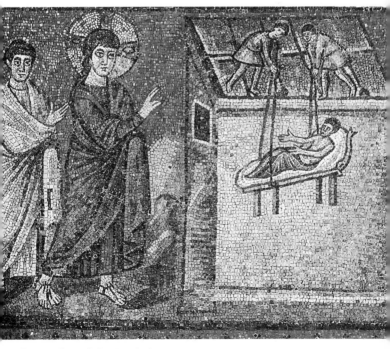

The Healing of the Paralytic. *Mosaic in S. Apollinare Nuovo, Ravenna.*

Detail from the Transfiguration *by Raphael.*

of matter. The gathered crowds cried out 'Hosanna' when they perceived half-consciously shining forth from him a radiance on his body as if it had become transparent for the spirit.

But five days later on Good Friday these same crowds cried out 'Crucify him, crucify him!' They were unable to see Christ for who he was.

Christ's suffering and death

Christ's passion actually began with the Baptism by John. The descent into and penetration of the earthly, physical realm could only mean pain for a spiritual being, who had no need out of himself to incarnate in a human body. His suffering increased with each step deeper into the fallen world of the physical human being. But this complete and total immersion in the fallen world of matter was necessary in order for God in Christ to overcome death. Because death could not be overcome from the outside, Christ had to come to the earth where death could take hold of him. Only then could God wrestle with and defeat death without interfering with the evolution of humanity.

But what is death? Seen from one point of view, death is the gap or abyss that opens up between spirit and matter. It is the threshold that must be traversed when we move from one realm to the other. At birth a kind of threshold is created which forms a bridge between this world and the world of spirit. Incarnated human beings are woven together of the physical and the spiritual. But in death the threshold becomes an abyss because the earth, the location of our I consciousness during life, is the realm from which the Father has withdrawn to leave us free. This abyss goes through the whole of creation, as a nothing, an emptiness. This is the place in the universe where the Father is not, but death is. In other words, death is the Father God who has withdrawn. The space left empty by the Father has become occupied by the prince of this world and humanity has been caught in his power in death and dying. When the prince of this world rules in this space, death means destruction. The mission of Christ was to replace the false form of death with its true form. When the place of death in this world is filled with Christ he shows us that, in reality, death is the source of eternal life.[21]

In traditional theological terms Christ took upon himself the earthly destiny of the human being: death. Originally, death was only a spiritual process. The Fall from paradise actually involved the awakened astral body. The desires of the astral body drew a veil in front of the spiritual world and tied the awakening I to the world of the senses. This was the spiritual death that led to the physical. So too, the overcoming of death must start from the spiritual. The I of Christ was so pure and strong that the astral body could not darken it or obscure its view of

the spiritual world. That is why Christ could carry his full I consciousness through death. And then, through the power of his spirit, he could re-create the human form of Jesus of Nazareth in its original purity. That was the Resurrection of Christ.

But before his Resurrection Christ descended into the realm of the dead. The apostle Peter said that Christ 'preached to those who are dead ...' (1Peter 4:6). This is known in traditional theology as the descent into hell. According to Steiner, Christ, after his victory over death, appeared in a part of the spiritual world where those who had died had become 'stuck' as it were, unable to continue further in their spiritual evolution. Having fallen prey to Ahriman such souls had become too attached to the earthly. At this time Christ once again set bounds to the power of Ahriman, lord of death in all its forms, so that in the future the experience of Man after death would be different.

What happened at the Resurrection?

When, as modern human beings we question what happened at the Resurrection, what we really want to know is what happened to the physical body. The question of the material substance of the Resurrection body is very complicated and dealt with in great detail in the eleven lectures Steiner gave in October of 1911.[22] The following is only a brief sketch.

As the earth 'precipitated' out of the spiritual world, becoming denser and ultimately material, the physical bodies of human beings were doing the same. Physical substance was becoming 'matter' as we know it. The process by which this took place meant pain and suffering for the spiritual beings out of which all substance is made. Concentration means pain. We can experience the connection between pain and concentration if we remember how pain and suffering focuses the mind, and, up to a certain point concentrates our consciousness. Of course, the

Christ in Limbo. *Woodcut by Albrecht Dürer.*

word 'substance' used for the spirit is a metaphor. There are no 'things' or even 'substances' in the spiritual world. That world is filled with *beings* who are characterized by their activities, by what they actually do. Their actions are really 'gestures of consciousness,' which can be said to have a certain form or shape.

Therefore, even when considered as a purely spiritual being, the human being has a form or shape. This form is very similar to what we call our physical body. Actually, it is the true *spiritual-physical* body. Owing to the Fall the true physical form-body, the originally invisible organism of flowing spiritual forces necessary to support human I-consciousness, has been 'filled in' with fallen matter. A process analogous to this occurs when iron filings 'fill in' and make visible the invisible, though physical, forces of magnetism. What we usually think of as the physical body is actually the *material-physical* body. By overcoming death and healing the flaw in the *spiritual-physical* body, Christ freed it from its dependency on the mortal earthly matter that it needed to maintain a human form on earth. When the original flaw in the human spiritual-physical body, the sting of death, was healed, then Christ no longer needed a *material* body to walk on the earth. Nevertheless, the Resurrection body was *physical*. It was spiritual-physical, having the shape and form of the human being. Furthermore, Christ was so sovereign in this body that he could 'condense' it to the point of tangibility for the disciple Thomas. He could also eat with the disciples and generally be as palpably present in the physical-material world as he wanted to be.

The transformation of the body of Jesus has meaning only if the true human form remains upright. This uprightness symbolizes the wakefulness, the consciousness of a human being who is self-contained and conscious of self. Hence, death on the cross was not arbitrary. The arms extended into the horizontal and the body held upright until death revealed the archetypical human form. When the nails were pounded in, the pain was intensified yet again and compressed his soul once more into

The Resurrection *by Grünewald.*

the body. This physical pain experienced by God himself enabled him to 'hold together' and meet death in full human-divine consciousness. The innocent, spiritual-physical body, perceptible through the veil of matter, was given power and substance through God's consciousness, enhanced by the pain of the wounds until death came. Then the sheaths began to separate as the blood of the sacrifice flowed down into the earth. But the power of 'concentration' given to Christ through the pain of the wounds permitted him to gather together the astral, etheric and physical bodies, to weave together — despite the presence and intentions of death (which are dis-integration, the absence of God) — the Resurrection body, the perfect human form, that will never have to die again.

Christ and the earth

The Resurrection was neither a miracle, in the sense of a magical breaking of the laws of nature, nor a deception. It is so difficult for us today to 'think' the Resurrection of Christ because our conception of the physical world and matter is so mechanical and simplistic. It usually does not occur to us that the laws of nature which are the expression of hardening processes, can also be reversed by the creative power of the Son God.

Yet, Steiner says, when the blood of Christ flowed into the ground of Golgotha the earth itself was changed and began to shine.

We know that in the material sphere a great quantity of fluid can be affected by the infusion of a very small quantity of a given substance. If you put a drop of some substance into a suitable fluid, it spreads through the fluid and colours the whole of it. In the material sphere, everyone understands this. But it is impossible to understand spiritual life if this principle is not understood in a spiritual sense. Our earth is not merely the material body we see with our eyes; it has a spiritual sheath. As we ourselves have an etheric body and an astral body, so the

Christ's Ascension *by Giotto.*

earth has such higher bodies. And just as a small quantity of substance spreads through a fluid, so that which rayed forth spiritually from the Act on Golgotha spread through the spiritual atmosphere of the earth, permeated it, and is still there. Something new has thus been imparted to our earth. And since souls do not merely live everywhere enclosed by matter, but are like drops in the seas of the earthly-spiritual, even so are human beings embedded in the spiritual atmosphere of our earth, which is permeated by the Christ-Impulse. That was not so before the Mystery of Golgotha, and it marks the great difference between pre-Christian and post-Christian life. If a person cannot imagine such a thing happening in

spiritual life, he is not yet far enough advanced to grasp
Christianity truly as a mystical fact, the full meaning of
which can be recognised and acknowledged only in the
spiritual world.[23]

Christ united himself with the earth itself and will be the
spirit of the earth and indwell it for all time. At the time of the
Christ's Resurrection, Lucifer and Ahriman had acquired great
power over the human physical body and the earthly substances
of which it is composed. There was a danger that humanity
might even die out because physical substance was becoming
too spiritually decadent to house a human soul and spirit. When
Christ united himself with the earth this danger ended because
he then united his own transformed life forces with those of the
earth. This last union happened at the Ascension. For forty days
the Resurrection body passed through a development becoming
ever more real and life-filled. Finally, imbued with the deepest
forces of the Father, it transcended the perceptual abilities of
the disciples and was withdrawn from their view. In the traditional Creed Christ is said to have gone 'to sit at the right hand
of the Father.' The 'right' hand traditionally symbolizing the
active, as opposed to the passive, receptive 'left' hand. This
means that Christ united with that part of the Father which
actively reaches into the world of earth. Because the relationship with the earth established through his death and Resurrection, Christ, now 'risen to heaven,' has the opportunity to
penetrate and transform the earthly world with the forces of
heaven.

Steiner said that when one seeks Christ today with supersensory sight that he is not found in the higher realms of heaven
but rather within the spiritual realms of earth. Christ's words to
the disciples, 'Lo, I am with you always, even unto the close of
the age' (Matt.28:20) mean that the earth is not a dead physical
body but is actually indwelled by Christ. The etheric body not
only of Man but of the earth is permeated by Christ and, as we
shall see in Chapter 4, the 'Second Coming' is related to this.

Although the earth is now the body of Christ it is not yet
completely spiritualized. Indeed, Christ will be suffering with

humanity until the earth is completely transformed into a spiritualized form at the end of earth evolution. At that time human beings will also dwell in spiritualized bodies similar to the Resurrection body of Christ.

The meaning of Whitsun

However, the attainment of a Resurrection body, that is, the salvation of human beings, will not take place automatically. Human beings are I-beings. Hence, they can only overcome death through a free deed of their own. But paradoxically, the human I, because of the Fall, is unable to do this.

The human I was given by God but it became infected by Lucifer who led the human being into a lower self and egotism. Since the Fall from paradise the human being has been living with a paradox in the core of his being. He did not create himself and yet he is independent. Although he is given freedom, still he cannot simply receive it; he must *be* it. This same paradox can also be expressed in terms of the I, which can never be 'possessed.' The desire to keep one's 'self' means to lose it. But the I can also be lost if someone merely subjects himself to the will of higher powers, leaving his destiny in their hands. Obedience to the will of a higher being is *not* the goal of humankind. Love for the ideal will lead us to act out of our innermost selves, out of 'Christ in us.' Our actions will then be in perfect harmony with the will of God but we will be doing what *we* want to do, not obeying any authority external to us. There will be no need to say 'Thy will be done' because then, God's will, will be my will and my will, God's will.

The life, death and Resurrection of Christ would not have been a deed of salvation for humanity if it were merely intended as a model, according to which we should conduct our lives. That alone would not be a great help. Real help can come to us because the I of Christ is related to the human self as Creator to creature. He is the divine being in whom every human I finds its primal ground. The fact that Christ's I is of like substance, though infinitely more powerful than ours, gives him

the possibility to help us from within. This idea is crucial for Rudolf Steiner's understanding of the essence of the human being and the true nature of redemption. Just as all creatures of God could only come into existence because the life of the Creator stands behind and yet lives within them, so too, all finite self-consciousness is carried by the divine 'I am,' in whose being it originates.

Being and not-being are present simultaneously in the human I on earth. The battle for equilibrium in this predicament is the human struggle. Christ brings the possibility of being a true I within this paradox. A personal relationship to Christ opens the way for a human being to say with Paul, 'Not I, but Christ in me,' (Galatians 2:20): but, of course, he says this *as an I*. Since Christ has entered into the realm of the earth we find in our souls a power which we cannot give ourselves. But we are not forced to make use of it. Two factors, however, work to encourage us to do so. One is Whitsun, the other is the fact of reincarnation and karma, to be dealt with in the next chapter.

With the descent of the Holy Spirit at Whitsun something entirely new begins: the archetype of a new kind of community, one that can include all of humanity. The disciples were gathered together and feeling entirely forlorn. It was the tenth day since Christ's Ascension into a realm which their spiritual perception could not reach. They experienced in their deep loneliness a profound movement in their souls and spirits. This stirred and brought to life memories of what they had experienced with Christ while he was on the physical plane both before and after the Resurrection. Then the words he had spoken to them illuminated these memories.

As a result of this rush of memories each disciple felt his individual connection with the Saviour. Their spiritual consciousness was awakened to the deeper meaning of all their experiences with him. They could see with spiritual insight and understand Christ's life, his deed and his being. They *knew* who he was through the power of the indwelling Spirit God, the Comforter, whom he had sent. The individual I of each was

Whitsun. *A miniature from an English psalter.*

filled with the Spirit. The tongues of spiritual fire were individual, one above each of the heads of the disciples. To truly grasp the message of the picture we need only imagine what it would have meant if there had been only one great fire hovering above the entire group.

The harmony of light-filled knowledge that filled their minds and hearts gave them the power to speak so that others were profoundly moved and able to understand them, no matter what their background or language. This is the model of the true Christian Church. Every individual I has a direct, personal relationship to Christ which allows it to be filled with the Holy Spirit. Wisdom from the Spirit God can take on a different form in each one of us; nevertheless harmony prevails because we are ultimately united in Christ and in the Spirit.

But for this Church to be realized the I's of human beings must be mature and Christ-filled. The ethical individualism Steiner presents in his basic ethical and epistemological work, *The Philosophy of Freedom,* is predicated on just this kind of maturity. The true I of each human being will bring forth its own ideas and all these ideas will be in harmony.

The Whitsun archetype for true Christian community quickly became obscured. The stage of development reached by humanity at the time of Christ did not yet allow for a widespread movement of such free communities. Initially, in order to deepen humanity's faith and love, Christianity had to be awakened in the heart and wills of human beings and less so in their thinking. This process reached its height in the Middle Ages when a full conscious understanding of the being of Christ was possessed by only a few initiates. Hence it was called esoteric or even occult. But the evolution of human consciousness has developed now to the point where our relationship to Christ depends as much on our power to think and understand as it does on the heart and will.

Today we must *comprehend* the mysteries of Christianity. Religious questions require answers arising out of an awareness and knowledge of higher worlds.

4. Reincarnation and karma

Sin and salvation

The traditional concepts of salvation and Christ as the saviour
of humankind have a place in the Christianity of Rudolf
Steiner; however, they are a part of a much larger understanding of humanity, the earth and the cosmos.

Salvation, to begin with, means overcoming the effects of
the Fall, the event in primeval times that caused the human
being's excess egotism and his flawed physical, etheric and
astral bodies. These flaws are the reason why we can think
wrong thoughts, have evil and ugly feelings, why human bodies
can become ill and ultimately must die. Taken together they
constitute what in traditional language was known as 'original
sin,' what Steiner referred to at times as the 'sickness of sin.'[24]

The Fall from paradise and its destructive effects extended
beyond the human realm. The expulsion from the garden of
Eden when the human physical body became material and
subject to death also marked the time when all of nature
became material and death-filled. Since the Fall, death pervades
all of the natural and human realms. 'All creation awaits
salvation,' as Paul said. It is still waiting.

With today's environmental awareness it is not difficult to
conceive of a sin against nature, but according to Steiner, *every
sin* has a component affecting nature. And nature, for Steiner,
is far more comprehensive than what today's nature-loving
materialist imagines. For behind the natural world of mountains,
rivers, the winds, trees, plants, and so on, there is a concrete
spiritual world. Elemental beings called sylphs, undines, sala-

manders, gnomes, and so on, live in and sustain nature.[25] These
and other nature beings are directly and profoundly affected by
the thoughts and feelings as well as the deeds of human beings
living in a geographical region. Good as well as evil thoughts
and feelings affect the life of nature profoundly. Decades later
this is then reflected in vegetation, wildlife and even the
weather.

Furthermore, the effects of human sin on the earth are
cumulative. According to Steiner, with our evil deeds we are
actually destroying the earth, the very place which ironically,
will become the arena of our own future evolution. Indeed, our
humanity is inextricably bound up with the earth itself and we
could not continue to evolve into the full humanity God intends
for us either as a species or as individuals, unless the earth is
habitable. Of course, our good deeds and thoughts also contrib-
ute to the creation of a future earth that will rise from the ashes
of the old.

The weight of sin through the ages would have already
destroyed the earth and with it our possibility of any future
existence as human beings were it not for the intervention of
God in the person of Christ Jesus. In uniting with the earth he
has taken on the consequences of human misdeeds which burden the earth. He is the one who 'takes away the sin of the
world.' When Christ says to the sick man in Chapter 9 of
Matthew's gospel 'Your sins are forgiven' this means, according to Steiner's interpretation, 'Christ has forgiven you so
completely that even the destructive spiritual consequences *for
the earth* have been eradicated.' What we by ourselves cannot
do — to undo the consequences of our sins for the earth —
Christ has done for him.

Repentance and destiny

There are, however, still consequences which human beings
must carry for themselves. These are consequences that God
would not take away from us. An immoral act not only
damages the earth, it also injures us in a way determined by the

nature of the deed. We are spiritually weakened and will only be able to grow strong again if we are confronted with the consequences. God sends us adversity in definite forms in order that we might have the opportunity to strengthen our souls in precisely those places where they are weak. The unfolding of this dynamic is known in traditional language as 'destiny.' The angels bring us what we need to grow inwardly. A term Steiner uses is 'karma.' What is here essential is that the personal consequences of our sins be transformed into destiny. To take away this aspect of sin would be to rob us of the possibility of advancement, ultimately, of salvation. Salvation cannot be a purely passive process or we would be robbed of our freedom. As we have seen, for Steiner freedom belongs to the essence of our humanity. Out of freedom we must decide to 'repent,' that is, to change our way of thinking so that we can discern the difference between good and evil, and begin to seek sources of strength for doing the good. Eventually we may come to recognize Jesus Christ as the one who can help.

However, our decision to follow Christ does not mean that the effects of the sickness of sin are immediately overcome in us, that we are 'saved.' Salvation has two elements: first of all, Christ's death, Resurrection, and Ascension were deeds which had consequences for all human beings. Every human being has already benefited from Christ's actions, whether or not he has ever heard of Christ Jesus. According to Steiner, the souls of human beings would not have been able to continue incarnating on earth were it not for Christ. And this aspect of Christ's coming provides the basis for a second element of salvation.

Christ in our weakness

Every human being must eventually come to the insight that the physical world is not all of reality, that the real meaning of life originates in another world. Having come to such a realization, we will ultimately be led by a destiny created by our guardian angel to seek to do the good. In this battle to do good and not evil we will often discover that we are completely powerless.

Full consciousness of this powerlessness will be like a death experience, a personal crucifixion of our highest ideals, of our higher self. In the pain of such moments Christ is able to come to us and our higher self will resurrect in the place where we say 'I' to ourselves. Our consciousness is a mixture of higher and lower self. The lower self and its selfishness leads to the death of the higher self again and again. As Steiner says, 'Christ is crucified everywhere in Man's lower nature.'[26] If we accept the truth, and do not avoid the pain but feel the suffering of that death, then Christ can give us the strength to rise again and again. With Christ's helping presence in our souls we can gradually transform the lower self.

But this kind of death and Resurrection cannot take place unless we are reaching for the good. We must be striving to follow the two commandments spoken of by Christ in Chapter 22 of Matthew's gospel with the words, 'You shall love the Lord your God with all your heart, and with all your soul and with all your mind,' and 'You shall love your neighbour as yourself.' The effort to follow those words of Christ will, if we are willing to face the death of our lower selves, inevitably lead us to Christ. This is essentially the same process described by St Paul in the Chapter 7 of his Letter to the Romans. For Steiner, a Christian would be someone who has consciously recognized Christ Jesus as the Lord, as the spiritual being to whom he or she can turn in prayer for help in the struggle to overcome the 'sickness of sin.'

In time the conscious struggle to overcome oneself and do the good, with Christ's help, will lead to a purification and transformation of the astral body, and then the etheric body, and ultimately the physical body, so that death will no longer exist. Salvation, then, is a long process that the human being can only achieve with the help of Christ, 'the Saviour.' This process is, indeed, such a long path that it requires more than one lifetime. We come here to the idea of reincarnation.

St Paul. Fourteenth-century mosaic from Istanbul.

Life after death

A description of how reincarnation works, in Steiner's view, must include a description of life before and after death. After death we are confronted with a giant panorama containing all the scenes from our life. All these memories, both conscious and unconscious, are recorded in the etheric body; with death they are freed from the physical and become visible to us. Standing, as it were, in the presence of Christ, we view our past life with utter objectivity and moral clarity. A moral resolve begins to form in our soul, to 'make up for' the false, ugly and evil deeds.

Some three and a half days after death, the etheric body dissolves into the spiritual world leaving only a tiny 'extract' which, in time, will form the basis for a physical body in the next incarnation. At this stage we consist of an I and an astral body as we move on to the next stage of post-earthly life called Kamaloca. Here there are two major experiences. Since we still possess our astral body we continue to experience the desires and emotions that dwell within it. Lacking a physical body through which they can be satisfied we experience deprivation in proportion to the degree of our attachment to the earthly. According to Steiner this results in a gradual 'burning out' of earthly desires, a purification of the soul from the merely earthly. In the old Christian tradition this 'burning' was attributed to 'hell' and understood as punishment for earthly misdeeds. The idea of Purgatory, a region where a soul is cleansed, is also a reflection of what Steiner describes as the true state of affairs.

The other experience in Kamaloca is that we live through our past life in reverse, from death to birth, while the soul feels *within itself* all the experiences that it caused other human beings and even animate and inanimate nature. All the joy and happiness as well as all the pain, humiliation, anger and

A tunnel of light, described by many as a near-death experience, depicted by Hieronymus Bosch in Ascent to the Empyrean.

suffering we have ever caused others comes streaming back to us; we experience these feelings as if we were the other. At this same time higher beings 'pass judgment' upon our earthly deeds. Good deeds are retained in the universe; bad ones must be compensated for, and as far as possible, be righted in later lives on earth.

The experience of Kamaloca provides the strongest possible incentive for us to want to do better in another life and to compensate others for the evil we have done them. It is important to realize here that the I itself *chooses* to compensate for its evil deeds on earth. The initiative stems from *us*, although the wisdom to know when and where to incarnate in order to find the conditions which will best shape our lives are given to us by higher beings.

After Kamaloca the astral body dissolves into the cosmos leaving an 'extract' that will form the basis for the creation of an etheric body in the following incarnation. Then the spiritual kernel of the human being, the I, moves outward and upward through successive realms of the spiritual world. This world has nothing in it of an external nature, nothing connected to the earth, but it is peopled with other human souls. Furthermore, we dwell in the 'atmosphere' of higher spiritual beings and are filled with their spiritual forces.

At the highest stage of our ascent we are in the presence of the Trinity. There, resting, so to speak, in the bosom of the Father, with no part of us manifested in any way outwardly we have an 'infinite inner life.' Then, a creative power begins to unfold in us and at this point furthest away from our past and future lives we experience a vision of all our previous earthly incarnations spread out before us like a tableau. At the same time a light appears from the future, the same light that illuminates our past. According to Steiner, this light is the Holy Spirit sent to us by Christ. This Spirit beckons us forward into the future. At this moment we finally make all those decisions that will take effect in the karma in the life before us. Contact with the Trinity has renewed the divine idea seeking realization through our I.

Life before birth and karma

As we again descend to earth we gather together the spiritual substance necessary to form our astral and etheric bodies which contain the results of all our previous lives. The total time between lives averages eight hundred to one thousand years, although there are many exceptions based on the karmic needs of individuals, communities, nations and the earth itself. Our path down to incarnation is guided by an angelic being who, before our earth evolution actually began, was entrusted with the task of guiding us through all our earthly incarnations. Traditional Christianity knows such beings as 'guardian angels.' They work together with the guardian angels of other people and higher hierarchies to plan the destinies of individuals, nations, peoples and the earth. With their wisdom we choose a generation, a country, a language and a family that will give us the hereditary possibilities and life experiences that will best enable us to meet our destiny. In sociological terms, heredity and environment are seen ultimately to have the same origin.

One of the last and most important experiences before incarnation is a prevision of the earthly life facing us in its general outline. Like a sketch that precedes the painting, we behold the life we have prepared for ourselves including all the compensations for former wrongs we now intend to right. We see too the opportunities that will be given to us to benefit humanity and the future of the earth.

Steiner said a great deal about the 'technique' of karma, about the particular kinds of situations we, together with angelic beings, create in our destinies.[27] There are many ways to pay back a karmic debt. Those who have united with Christ will be able to 'work off' their karma with deeds that go far beyond the repayment of any debt. Their deeds will help others with their debt and bring blessing to the earth itself.

We are guided by spiritual beings who lead us to develop strengths where before we were weak, to meet people whom we 'owe' and to meet people who 'owe' us. Nevertheless, we are still left free. It is still possible for us to turn our back on the lessons that we, in our higher selves, want to learn. However, this would mean that our suffering would only increase and take different forms in future lives. On the other hand accepting one's sacrifices and suffering as 'God given' actually draws one closer to Christ, who is everywhere present in the spiritual atmosphere of the earth, waiting to help human souls who turn to him. According to Steiner, Christ has united with the higher self of every human being, whether or not they are conscious of it. Hence, to accept the destiny intended for us by our higher selves and prepared for us by our guardian angels, is to unite with the will of Christ, making it possible for him to strengthen and comfort. The old adage that 'God never gives us a destiny which is beyond our strength,' is supported and made understandable by realizing that the strength we need only comes to us once we have truly accepted that our fate actually originates in Christ's will for our salvation.

Of course, this does not mean we should not struggle to help others who are suffering, to better our own or other people's lives. Anthroposophic teaching concerning karma does not advocate simple resignation to what is. It provides the basis for a deeper understanding of life and its problems and helps us begin to find the wisdom for which St Francis prayed: to know the difference between what can be changed and what cannot be changed.

Furthermore, it *is* possible to help others with the burden of their karma. Even those individuals who have fully paid off their own personal karmic debt would, in the spirit of Christ, continue to incarnate rather than remain in heaven. As long as there are human souls on earth in chains, either spiritual, soul or physical, they will not be happy. Just as Christ took upon himself the karma of humanity by freely uniting with the earth and its destiny, so too a perfected human being would return to earth to help with the karma of others. Christ himself, however, does not reincarnate. His mission required that he live in an earthly body only once in order to unite with mankind and the earth. Living as he does now in the spiritual atmosphere of the earth, he never really leaves the earth to ascend as a deceased human being would, to the Father God in the heights of the spiritual world. Not only does he himself not need to incarnate again on the earth but furthermore, humanity would not benefit from it.

The idea of reincarnation has implications for many theological problems which traditional Christianity finds extraordinarily difficult. An individual who is born into a culture where the idea of Jesus Christ has never appeared has not lost the opportunity for 'eternal salvation.' A special relationship to the divine is possible in every culture in the world. It may well be the destiny of an individual to absorb other, non-western religions in any particular incarnation.

Additionally, the souls who lived on the earth before Christ did not miss the opportunity to know him. Those same souls have been born since Christ. Children who have died before becoming old enough to consciously find Christ for themselves have not missed their chance for 'salvation.' They are rather human beings who have already just lived a full lifetime and needed, for some special reason, only to be born again and live a short while. Or they will soon be born again and be given the opportunity to live a full life.

Abortion considered as a religious question also looks different in the light of reincarnation. A foetus is not just a collection of cells. Behind it is a human being with a destiny who seeks to be born to a particular mother and father at a particular time and place. One human being is coming to another. Souls who are aborted while attempting to be born are being told, in effect, 'I do not want you.' Of course, such souls will try again and may have to settle for being born somewhere else on the earth. Then, with the help of the angels, they will try somehow to meet up with those people in their karma who rejected them.

This is far more complicated than simply saying that abortion is right or wrong. It is a way of understanding concretely the spiritual consequences of our actions. A woman with ten children and no way of supporting them may decide that the eleventh child will have to find himself another family. From some points of view such a decision will, of course, be right. But more importantly than right or wrong is the fact that consequences will follow. If a mistake has been made, if someone has been wronged, the one making the decision will one day have to make it up to him. A society that allows millions of unborn souls to be sent back into the spiritual world to 'try again' will also suffer consequences. In such cases we can speak of the karma of a community and individuals who have no responsibility for causing the karmic effects must also help bear the consequences for all of society.

The Second Coming of Christ

There is a great deal that belongs to an individual simply because he lives at a particular time and in a particular community. We incarnate again and again because the earth and the humanity on it is evolving. Each incarnation gives us an opportunity to experience a different kind of consciousness. History is actually the history of evolving human consciousness. In the distant past we perceived spiritual beings because of the nature of the bodies we lived in. They were more porous for the spirit, not yet so deeply united with the earth. In the future we will again begin to perceive spiritual beings. According to Steiner, the event known in the Bible as the Second Coming of Christ actually comes about when humanity evolves to the point where individuals are no longer so attached to, and limited by the physical, material earth that they can see only the physical world. They will gradually begin to perceive beings and events in the etheric world, also known as the sphere of life, that sphere of the spiritual world directly bordering on the earthly. Christ dwells in this world, in 'the realm of the clouds,' as it is imaginatively referred to in the second chapter of Acts of the Apostles. Starting in the twentieth century the process of being 'lifted out' or 'up' into the realm of the etheric will increasingly affect every human being over the course of the future millennium. Those who are prepared will recognize what they see. Others will suffer enormous soul pain and disorientation until they understand. This Second Coming of Christ is not what is called in the Apocalypse the final judgment. That awaits a much later age. But there is a judgmental element in the etheric appearance of Christ. Those who have lived in such a way that they do not recognize him will be judged by their own lack of understanding. But this judgment will lead them to new experiences which will show them a path into the future.

5. Men, women and the gender of God

'The universal human being'

The ideal of a perfect human being embraces both sexes, all nationalities, races and ethnic groups while reflecting the unique contributions of each. This ideal is a spiritual archetype of 'the universal human being.' All the different ways of being human provide opportunities for developing toward this universal ideal. However, as a consequence of the Fall we are all tempted to base our judgments of others upon superficial physical or soul characteristics and lose sight of their deeper spiritual nature, that is, their fundamental connection at a *spiritual level*, to 'the universal human being.' Rudolf Steiner recognizes this temptation in his first major work, *The Philosophy of Freedom*, in the chapter titled 'The Individual and Genus.' After a critique of the limitations of judging human beings according to their national traits, and so on, he writes what could have been the platform for the feminist movement:

> The tendency to judge according to the genus is at its most stubborn where we are concerned with differences of sex. Almost invariably man sees in woman, and woman in man, too much of the general character of the other sex and too little of what is individual. In practical life this does less harm to men than to women. The social position of women is for the most part such an unworthy one because in so many respects it is determined not as it should be by the particular characteristics of the individual woman, but by the general picture one

has of woman's natural tasks and needs. ... What a
woman ... wants to become had better be left to the
woman herself to decide. If it is true that women are
suited only to that profession which is theirs at present,
then they will hardly have it in them to attain any other.
But they must be allowed to decide for themselves what
is in accordance with their nature. To all who fear an
upheaval of our social structure through accepting
women as individuals and not as females, we must reply
that a social structure in which the status of one half of
humanity is unworthy of a human being is itself in great
need of improvement.[28]

The reader will see from this that the following characteriza-
tions of typical masculine and feminine soul characteristics are
not derived from social norms, but are to be read in the light of
'the universal human being.'

Masculine and feminine soul constitutions

The words of Genesis 1:27, that 'God created man, male and
female,' means, according to Steiner, that the original human
being had both the masculine and the feminine aspects united
within him. The separation into the two sexes, which did not
occur until later was soon followed by the Fall. Although a
tragedy, the Fall was a necessary step that resulted not only in
death, but also in knowledge and the power of creation, both
sexual and otherwise. As we saw in Chapter 3, it also led ultimately to the power of love and freedom.

In the third chapter of Genesis we hear God speak of Eve
bearing children in pain and Adam working on the earth in
order to eat. As we have already seen they are actually words
of blessing, for they describe the activities that will ultimately
lead humankind back to heaven. The meaning of pain is to
bring forth new life, to awaken a new human being within us.
The words were spoken to Eve because the feminine aspect of
the human soul, whether in a man or a woman, is that which

can endure pain fruitfully. The work of Adam, whether done by a man or a woman, is to transform the earth. Since the Fall all human beings, men and women alike, must bear pain and work.

The I, the purely spiritual kernel of the human being, is of the same spiritual substance in both men and women. Thus men and women are spiritually equal. Men and women are, however, constituted somewhat differently. The relationships between the I, the astral, etheric and physical bodies are different. The spirit is the same in men and women but the soul realm, and obviously the physical, are constituted differently. The minds of men and women can grasp the same spiritual truths and live in the same reality but they may arrive at their thoughts through different paths in their souls. This means that men and women relate to the world differently.

According to Steiner the spirit works into the woman generally more through the feeling aspect of the soul and in the man generally more through the will. This means that the woman tends to experience meaning first in her feelings and intuitions, which must then be raised to conscious thought for full clarity. Men, on the other hand, experience meaning first in their will, a realm with even less consciousness. They often need to have their actions reflected back to them by others before they can become conscious of the meaning behind their intentions. When the will of a human being unfolds in thinking itself the result is a fortunate event for the individual and humanity *unless* the person loses touch with his feelings and the concrete world around him. Without sufficient feelings, he easily becomes lost in intellectual abstractions and produces ideas dangerous to humankind; and this is more of a danger with men.

The particular constitution of women tends to protect them when thinking, from losing touch in the way men often do. When women bring their thinking and willing together the result is a fortunate event *unless* she is unable to free herself from the merely personal element in feelings. Too much subjectivity is the temptation women must usually overcome. In Steiner's terminology men are more tempted by Ahriman, women by Lucifer; women tend not to be deeply enough incarnated, men are more often too deeply incarnated for their own good.

However, we must remember that these differences are merely averages. There are women who can relate to the world the same way as men and men who can relate to the world in the same way as women. Like race, temperament and language, gender is one of the layers of soul clothing we must wear in order to live on the earth and struggle through to the universal human. The spiritual human-I, the true human archetype, is above all polarities. Indeed the I uses the polarity to grow. It is the tension between the two poles within us and between us and others that makes creativity and evolution possible.

To be a complete human being we each need both poles, which are a reflection of the great cosmic polarity of the universe: yin and yang, passive receptivity and active initiative, perception and thinking.

T'ai-chi T'u diagram, expressing the interaction of yin and yang.

For this reason, according to Steiner, we usually reincarnate alternating sexes, to balance out our one-sided experience of a previous lifetime. This idea also casts a new light on the psychology of hatred of the opposite sex. People who are unable to ever see anything but the worst traits of the opposite sex may still be reacting with disgust to their *own* excesses in a previous lifetime.

Why God the Father? — cosmic rhythms

The spiritual equality of masculine and feminine ways of being does not mean that they must both be equally manifested at the same time. At any given moment either one or the other may be required to advance our personal or humankind's spiritual evolution. There are times when we must speak and times when we must listen to what comes back to us. All life, including spiritual life unfolds in rhythms. The active and the passive come into play in turn. Every new phase begins with an out-going masculine, active initiating stage followed by an inner, feminine, consolidating, reflecting, stage that provides the 'mother ground' for the next phase.

This rhythmical unfolding manifests in the history of the created universe as well. Although the Godhead is entirely above the male-female duality, it contains within it, in undiffer-entiated harmony, the essence of masculinity and femininity. Out of this wholeness there rose up the impulse to act, the initiative required to start something entirely new, to create something where there had been nothing before. This impulse represents that part of the Godhead which could be called masculine. It could be called the outbreathing of the Word, of divine substance. The feminine aspect of the Godhead, as an essential part of the undifferentiated whole, was also present at the beginning. After a phase of manifestation and development, the results of evolution are taken back into the Godhead. This is the feminine in-gathering, and inner reflection on the active phase. The entire earth evolution as we know it represents the largest 'masculine-feminine' cycle of evolution we can imagine: a period of materialization, manifestation and history followed by a gradual dematerialization and spiritualization. In the sec-ond, 'feminine' phase, the souls of human beings will mature, reflecting on and consolidating the earthly achievements that can carry on into eternity. This stage will culminate in the great 'interval of rest' as Steiner calls it, between earth evolution and the stage known as the New Jerusalem, or 'Jupiter' incarnation of earth.[29]

On earth both masculine and feminine divinities have been experienced and worshipped at different times depending on what was needed for the further development of the worshipping community. In Lemurian and Atlantean times the motherly aspect of the Godhead was of the greatest importance for humankind. But the fatherly aspect of God was required to develop the human I because the essence of the I is inner initiative. Although the spiritual substance of the human self can be given from without, it is only unconscious, only potential, until it awakens and thereby *creates itself* as an I-being through its own inner initiative.

Monotheism was also needed because the human 'I' needs to experience a divine 'Thou' in order to have a consolidated divine reflection of itself as one. This divine 'masculine' 'Thou' was and is experienced as the Lord and Father in heaven. Hence, we had the impulse-filled, warlike 'Aryan sky gods' appearing on the theatre of world religions leading up to the God of Abraham, Isaac and Jacob. Patriarchy on earth was a reflection, often distorted, as are all earthly reflections, of what was spiritually necessary for the birth of the self. The Indo-European languages have been another tool used by spiritual beings to focus the earthly experience of the self. They all use the masculine forms of pronouns to designate a human being whose gender is unspecified. English as the most Western of Western languages even uses 'man' to mean 'member of the human race' independent of sex.

Until our age the guidance and evolution of language has been entirely in the hands of archangels.[30] These beings used Shakespeare, Goethe, Dante, Cervantes and other such geniuses to shape and mould language so that human beings could perceive and develop thoughts about the world of heaven and earth in a way appropriate for their time. When we take hold of language and consciously attempt to improve upon it we should bear in mind the great responsibility we take upon ourselves.

Biblical imagery

In the Old Testament God is portrayed as extremely masculine.
He is depicted as judge and punisher of sinners. It is not until
the New Testament that we find a picture of God that truly
supplements the masculine with a feminine side. The story of
the prodigal son shows us a Father who is not judging and
punishing but comforting, understanding, forgiving and helpful.
These feminine characteristics are also reflected in John's Apocalypse in the words, 'He will wipe away every tear from their
eyes.' These and other words from the New Testament indicate
that God has 'motherly' as well as 'fatherly' characteristics.
The most motherly characteristic of the Godhead is seen in the
image of the Son God being born out of the substance of the
Father. This is the motherly 'gift of life,' the sacrificial and
nurturing aspect of the Godhead manifested through the Father.

God himself as Christ, the Son God, shows in his two
aspects, the Lion of Judah and the sacrificial Lamb of God, a
complete union of the masculine and feminine poles. Only in
this case the sequence is reversed. The death on the cross is the
passive, feminine sacrifice that makes possible the ensuing,
active battle with death, the more masculine aspect, necessary
for Resurrection. The Lamb becomes the Lion. In the second
half of earth evolution, which began with Christ's death and
Resurrection, the eternal feminine aspect of the human soul
again increasingly comes into play.

These two aspects of our humanity are also seen in the biblical imagery of the 'kings of the earth' and the 'Bride of Christ.'
To become a conscious I-being *on the earth,* every human
being must become a 'king,' a *man* who can rule. Yet, to move
beyond the stage of the lower self, however well perfected, the
human being must go on to purify his soul in the selfless pur-
suit of knowledge and in selfless deeds of love so that he can
also become the 'Bride of Christ,' a *woman* who can give birth
to a child.

The imagery of the marriage describes the union of the
earthly human soul with the heavenly bridegroom, the Christ.

Sophia. From a seventeenth-century manuscript.

Occasionally in the past, and increasingly in the future, the divine Sophia with her emphasis on purity and wisdom, is sent like an angel, to help individual human beings with this transformation of soul forces. But we must first become individuals before she can help.[31] Furthermore, it is not certain that this marriage will take place. The 'kings' of the earth must face temptation from the 'whore of Babylon' described in Chapters 17 and 18 of the Book of Revelation. They can use their 'self-possessed' soul forces to wallow in the pleasures of the sense world, a world which, in cosmic terms at least, will soon pass away. Therefore, it is a dead end for humanity. The physical-material sense world is here to teach us.

As we learn to love the world *and* to know it for what it is,

we also discover the pleasures it can give us. Uniting ourselves
with it in an impure, egotistical fashion could lead to our
experiencing 'the death of matter.' This would mean that the
creative forces needed to give birth to a higher, eternal self are
dissipated in sensual excess and surrender of self to 'Babylon
the great, mother of harlots and of earth's abominations.'
(Revelation 17:5) Yet it is important to bear in mind that the
earth itself is not the temptation; it is the possibility of our
impure relationship that can lead us astray.

As a result of the 'masculine' initiating influence from the
spiritual world, the lower self, which is like a place holder for
the higher self, has learned to create and assert itself. Yet the
ultimate reason for our developing this lower self with its
wakeful self-consciousness is to sacrifice it for others. Only
such a sacrifice allows Christ to enter the soul and fill it with
its true divine content. Then we can act with the strength of the
earthly self for divine purposes, for the benefit of others.
Human beings who do not learn to make this sacrifice and
ground their sense of self in something other than the earthly
will themselves lose any sense of self when the earthly passes
away.

The human soul and the divine Sophia

In the Trinity the feminine aspect of the Godhead is represented
by the Holy Spirit. In a lecture Rudolf Steiner said:

> We can represent what lives in the soul under two
> aspects: the aspect of sensation, the great impulse giver,
> the great fructifier; then there is what illuminates the
> soul as ideation and mental pictures; this is the part of
> the soul at rest which receives its content from outside.
> The soul at rest which allows itself to be fructified by
> impressions from the world, is the Mother. The sum of
> sensations through the universe is the masculine in the
> soul, the Father. That which allows itself to be fructified
> is the feminine in the soul, the Mother in the soul, the

eternal feminine. That through which the human being
becomes conscious of himself is called by the mystic,
the Son.

The aspects of the soul are: Father, Mother, Son.
They correspond to the three aspects in the cosmos:
Father, Son and Spirit, the three aspects of the spirit of
the world.[32]

That part of the soul which allows ideation — thinking
thoughts, entertaining mental pictures — is the 'mother' part of
the human soul, that which corresponds to the Spirit God. In
other places,[33] he describes this part of the soul as the astral
body and says further that when the astral body has been
completely purified it is called in esoteric language 'the Virgin
Sophia.' In that condition it can be fructified by the Holy Spirit.
The result is not only the birth of the higher self but also
spiritual enlightenment.

Now and in the future we will be called upon increasingly
to experience the world through our feminine side if we wish
to make progress. This could mean, for example, not always
reaching out to change the world immediately when suffering
comes to us, but living with the pain long enough to hear what
it has to teach us before acting.

Of course, the masculine side of the human being, in the
process of development for the past five thousand years must
not be discarded. Properly developed through many incarnations, it leads to the dignity and independence of a unique
human self, of our own I. Patriarchy, which made this possible,
is growing less significant, and is even in large measure out-
moded as a means for advancing humankind in Western
societies. As we have seen, something good at one point in time
can become evil if it outlasts its purpose. But it is also true that
a spiritual impulse appropriate for the future can work destruc-
tively if forced into incarnation too early. According to Steiner
the full revelation of the spiritual forces of the divine Sophia
will only occur for humanity in general during the sixth post-
Atlantean epoch.[34] This era will not begin for approximately
another fifteen hundred years. That epoch will see the spiritual

development of the astral body into 'Manas,' or 'Spirit-Self,' which will make human beings particularly ripe for inspiration from the Holy Spirit through the Sophia.[35]

There are those today inspired by the intuition that a special relationship to the feminine aspect of God awaits us. Yet because it is so many centuries before such an experience is entirely appropriate for all of humankind, current attempts to worship feminine divine beings are often merely revivals of ancient forms appropriate to a time before the human I was born. It is possible today to surrender the conscious human self to nature or other spirits in order to experience the body, or nature itself, as sacred. However, the question must be asked, 'Which divine feminine presence are we then dealing with?' As we have seen from the Book of Revelation, 'the feminine' can also offer experiences which are not beneficial to humankind.

An evolutionary perspective on women's spirituality

Evil can approach us from two directions: as something from the past that tries to last too long and as something from the future that tries to appear too early. In the middle we must try to discern and create what is appropriate for our particular age. We are aided in this by Steiner's evolutionary perspective on the human relationship to the spirit differentiated by gender. For example, women, who are generally less deeply incarnated than men, in ancient times could be more easily overwhelmed by spiritual beings who wished to use them for their own purposes. When this happened the woman was actually possessed; her I was extinguished for a time. When deeply moved by religious experience women were in greater danger than men of being 'lifted out' and involuntarily providing a gateway for any spirit wishing to push its way in. This is why Paul said women should cover their heads in Church and not speak. Paul's healing of the slave girl possessed by a spirit of divination (Acts 16) is an example. The presence of Christ in Paul, the closeness of the true I of every human being, drew the girl back into her soul so there was no place for foreign spirits. The girl was healed and liberated to herself.

In the almost two thousand years since Paul wrote his letters humankind has fallen much deeper into matter; both men and women are more deeply incarnated. The I's of women are now firmly anchored in their souls while the I's of men have become so deeply sunk into their bodies that it is extremely difficult for them to think spiritual thoughts except under special circumstances. Women today can not only speak in churches, they can become priests. A modern priest works out of his or her I, the centre of his or her humanity, not out of maleness or femaleness.

In the future, incarnations as women will take on an even greater significance for humanity's spiritual evolution. Steiner explained why almost all of the past incarnations of important people were as men. He said,

> I stress the point here that I am not considering the female incarnations because, in the past, life as a man was more important. Incarnations as women are only now beginning to be of importance. In the future it will be of quite particular interest to take precisely the female incarnations into account.[36]

The feminine aspect of the Father God is seen in his motherly aspects, specifically his giving birth to the Son God. The feminine aspect of the Son God is seen in his empathy, compassion and ultimately his sacrifice for humankind. But when we come to the Spirit God we find a special manifestation of the feminine aspect of the Godhead. The figure of Mary, the mother of Jesus has long been connected with the appearance of the Spirit. Mary was filled with the Holy Spirit and manifested him in her purity. We see in her and all the legends surrounding her how the Spirit brings not only meaning and knowledge, but also purity, grace, beauty, harmony, imagination, and dignity. Steiner also spoke of other manifestations of the eternal feminine, the divine Sophia, for example, who is also a reflection of the Holy Spirit and represents another side

of Mary. Ancient Judaism in the Wisdom Books of the Old
Testament Apocrypha speaks of 'Sophia' (Greek for 'wisdom')
and Chochmah (Hebrew for 'wisdom'), as feminine beings who
worked with God at the creation. In the Wisdom of Solomon,
Sophia is herself 'mother,' (7:12), sits by God's throne (9:4)
and can do all things (7:27).

The masculine-feminine polarity lives in dynamic harmony
in all three persons of the Trinity. Working in harmony with
great rhythms of earthly evolution, the Godhead reveals in
different planetary incarnations and epochs more the masculine
or the feminine forces contained in the Trinity. Human beings
worshipping God on earth are shaped by these forces according
to what is needful in any given epoch on the way to evolving
into the ideal, the universal, human being.

6. Religion and the future of the earth

Religion

Rudolf Steiner had much to say about the practice of Christianity both individual and communal. Most importantly he stressed the need for modern human beings to understand Christianity. In 1906 Steiner wrote:

> Humanity is presently at a stage of development, where a large portion of it would lose all religion, if the higher truths that underpin it are not proclaimed in a form that can be seen as valid to the sharpest reflection. The religions are true but for many people the time is past when it was possible to understand through mere faith. ... If the truth and wisdom that underlie religious ideas are not proclaimed in public in a form that can stand up to thorough thinking, then there will be an immediate invasion of doubt and loss of faith. And an era in which this is the case, would be worse off than an era of barbarism, despite all its material culture. One who knows the real conditions of human life, knows that as much as it is impossible for a plant to live without its nourishing sap it is also impossible for a human being to live without any relationship to the invisible world.[37]

Religion itself Steiner regarded as a 'feeling for, or an experience of, the mood of the eternal.' He said:

> Following the way people have attempted to bring religion into the stream of humanity in recent centuries,

religion is a combination of two things; one of which
should not really be called religion in the strict sense of
the word; the other *is* religion.'[38]

He meant that philosophizing about religion is not religion. He
said further, 'the more we can intensify this feeling for or mood
of, eternity, the more we advance religion in us or other
people.'[39]

Religion, then, according to Steiner is not the propagation of
certain teachings but the cultivation of certain feelings. Faith is
not the holding of certain ideas to be true but an experience in
the human heart, an experience of one's connection with God.
And because of the significance of thinking for our age, ideas
can aid or hinder religion.

Although Steiner himself was a deeply religious man, and
spoke about spiritual worlds and spiritual beings — at times
with very great feeling — he was, nevertheless, speaking out of
knowledge. Yet he made a sharp distinction between the
practice of anthroposophy and religion itself. For those of his
followers able only to understand the results of spiritual science
and not to produce results themselves, the temptation to simply
receive Steiner's words as revelation and to make a religion out
of anthroposophy is very great. In recognition of this problem
Steiner often said that his words should not simply be believed
or in anyway be made into a dogma, religious or otherwise. To
counteract this tendency he said in 1917:

At this point I believe I ought to make an insertion
which is important and which really should be well
understood, particularly by the friends of our spiritual
science. The matter should not be represented as if spiritual scientific endeavours were intended as a substitute
for the life and practice of religion. Spiritual science can
in the highest degree, and particularly concerning the
mystery of Christ, be a support, a foundation for the life
and practice of religion. But spiritual science should not
be made into a religion; but one ought to be clear that
religion in its active life and living practice within the

human community kindles the spirit-consciousness of the soul. If this spiritual consciousness is to come alive in man, he cannot remain content with abstract representations of God or Christ but will have to involve himself again and again in the practice of religion, in religious activity, which for every individual can take on a different form ...[40]

Prayer and meditation

Religious activity can include the individual practice of prayer and meditation, subjects concerning which Steiner had a great deal to say. Religion is usually thought of primarily as an activity that meets the personal, subjective need of individual men and women, that is, it exists merely to benefit human beings. But according to Steiner, spiritual beings actually need human beings praying on the earth. They need them not only because such human beings thereby make themselves more open to insights from the spiritual world, but also because the spiritual substance created by the prayer and meditation of human beings is precious to, and needed by heaven in many ways. For example, our thoughts and prayers can create forms in the astral world that actually nourish departed souls. One of the results of our prayer for other people is the creation of a spiritual substance that can be taken up by angels and used to assist the person for whom we praying. Our conscious activity on the earth has definite consequences for heaven.

In prayer we address a spiritual being and lift our soul to them. In meditation we concentrate our thinking and thereby develop structures within our soul which eventually enable us to *perceive* in the spiritual world. Furthermore, prayer and meditation are by no means exclusive categories. Steiner sometimes speaks of meditative prayer or prayerful meditation. Both involve thinking, feeling and willing. However, the stress is placed more on thinking and willing in meditation and the will and feeling in prayer. Meditation, as Steiner conceived it, was an activity carried out by individuals. The conscious human I working on its own 'sheaths,' transforming them for spiritual development. Because the results of such transformation must be under the control of the individual I, it would be wrong, even dangerous for one human being to meditate for another. For this reason Steiner gave no 'group meditations' whereby physical presence in a group made progress possible for some individuals who otherwise might not advance. However, he did give the same meditation to groups who, meditating on their own as individuals at different times and locations, thereby create a 'spiritual vessel' to receive from higher spiritual beings insight and strength intended to help the group with its spiritual task on the earth. But in such cases it is essential to remember that the individuals meditate alone.

Meditation and prayer are willed activities that attract the attention of spiritual beings, both good and bad. The good are drawn to a striving human being whom they then seek to help; the bad are attracted to a striving human being whom they attempt to distract through temptations. According to Steiner, if meditation is not done properly there is a danger of a one-sided development of the soul which is soon taken advantage of by the adversaries to thwart our development. He constantly stressed that three steps must be taken in moral development for every step in spiritual development.

The significance of ritual and myth

Prayer is a spiritual activity that can be done not only alone but also in groups. Furthermore, the ceremonies carried out in such religious communities bear a special relationship to the spiritual world:

> In their ceremonies, sacraments and rites the various
> religions have presented externally visible pictures of
> higher spiritual events and beings. Only someone
> who has not yet thoroughly understood the depths of
> the great religions cannot know this. But someone who
> can see into spiritual reality himself will also under-

stand the great significance of these externally visible acts.[41]

In many lectures he described the inner side of these 'externally visible acts' in detail as, for example, when speaking of the Eucharist, Christ's Last Supper with the disciples and how Christ can be present in bread and wine. But our age with its abstract, literal thinking finds it very hard to take myth and sacramentalism seriously. Some modern forms of Christianity have completely done away with all ritual, others have 'watered down' the sacraments in an effort to bring them closer to the souls of human beings living in a secular age. The materialistic assumptions behind modern interpretations of scripture have led to absurd and condescending judgments concerning the Bible. In a lecture from 1908, Steiner said:

> It is our purpose to show that there were, at one time, wholly spiritual interpretations of biblical documents and that when the materialistic tendency arose, it read into the Bible what is now objected to by liberal minded people. The materialistically inclined mind first created what it then itself later opposed.[42]

As a result of this 'reading into' we have seen the 'demythologizing' of the Gospels and, indeed, of all religious creeds from the past. Of course, if the Resurrection were just a 'myth,' unbelievable to modern minds, then we must confine ourselves to the moral teachings of 'the simple Man of Nazareth.' Such is the theological understanding of many at the present time. The abstract, materialistic rationalism of the previous three centuries prevents many from thinking of the spirit in any way that is both concrete and spiritual.

The Christian Community

In response to requests Steiner held a series of lectures in June and October of 1921 in which he presented the fundamentals of how a Christian Church could function in the modern age. He explained the need for sacraments in religion. According to him the great stress on sermons and 'the simple word' in Protestant churches has lead to the atomization of congregations. In a time when humanity consciously 'takes in' reality primarily through the senses it is essential that men and women also be able to perceive, within 'sensual reality,' perfect reflections of spiritual reality. The forms perceptible in true ritual provide a door for spiritual beings to enter the souls of human beings on the earth. A Christian Church today needs the power of the sacraments. Steiner also said:

> In times to come an initiate will be able to say to his pupils: When you participate truly in a sacred enactment of cult or ritual, you are engaged in something of which the materialist says that it has no reality, or, if he is a cynic, he will say that it is all child's play. Nevertheless, the enactments of a true rite contain spiritual power. The elementary spiritual beings who are evoked when such a rite is enacted, have need of the rite because from it they draw nourishment and forces of growth.
>
> As I have said, a time will come when the material substance in minerals, plants, animals, clouds, the forces working in wind and weather and also, of course, all the accoutrements used in rites and ceremonies, will pass away, will be dissipated in the universe. But the spiritual beings who have been called down into the sphere of the rites and sacred enactments — these will remain when the earth approaches its end. They will remain, in a state of more perfect development, within the earth, just as in autumn the seed of next year's plant is concealed within the present plant, so the substance in the mineral, plant and animal kingdoms will disintegrate in the universe, but the perfected elementary beings will be there, living on into the Jupiter existence as a seed of the future.
>
> I have said many times: The kingdom of plants, of animals, of minerals, all that lives in wind and storm, in clouds — even the radiance of the stars — will be dis-

persed and scattered; not one particle will remain. But what man prepares spiritually — this *will* remain.[43]

In Steiner's view, sacred enactments, along with all forms of genuine prayer and meditation, are one of the powerful means by which the earth and the beings that stand behind it are spiritualized and transformed. 'Jupiter existence' is a term Steiner sometimes used to designate the future state of the earth called the 'New Jerusalem' in the Book of Revelation. It will be a spiritual world lacking matter as we know it.

Recognizing the inadequacies of modern theology and the plight of institutional Christianity, a number of young anthroposophists approached Steiner with the question whether he regarded an independent movement for the renewal of religion desirable or necessary. Steiner replied that he had hoped a sufficient number of priests and ministers in the existing churches might become interested in anthroposophy and thereby renew the Christian Church. Since that had not happened, however, then it would be possible, if a sufficient number of suitable people were interested, to found an independent movement, intended as a renewal of the Christian Church. He stressed, however, that it was not *his* task to found churches or religions and that they would have to do this themselves. He was prepared to offer them all the help they needed; but the initiative, the 'spiritual responsibility' for such a deed must come from others.

Led by Friedrich Rittelmeyer, a well-known pastor and author in the German Lutheran Church, forty-five mostly young men and women (it was clear to all from the beginning that women would participate fully as priests) founded the priesthood of The Christian Community, Movement for Religious Renewal, in 1922 in Dornach, Switzerland. The founders had heard Steiner describe the sacraments in their sevenfold aspect. He also discussed the essentials of a renewed theology, of a deepened and enriched pastoral care and community life. His listeners were astonished by his knowledge of theology and its history, by his masterly handling of even the most practical questions of congregational life. Complete freedom of thought

Friedrich Rittelmeyer (1872–1938)

as well as belief in the full cosmic reality of the sacraments were united in this new movement. What priests or members speak or write in The Christian Community is done on their own personal authority. They have the freedom to teach anything that accords with the sacraments. Members are not required to accept any official theology. The desire to become a member grows out of an experience of Christ's blessing presence in the sacraments.

The Christian Community consists of interdependent but free congregations spread throughout the world whose community life is centred around the traditional seven sacraments in renewed form. The sacrament of bread and wine, the Commu-

*Emil Bock
(1895–1959),
founder
priest and
later leader
of The
Christian
Community.*

nion, is celebrated with a new name, the Act of Consecration
of Man, indicating the goal of life on earth: to become true
human beings. The other six sacraments of The Christian Community include: the Baptism of children, Confirmation, Sacramental Consultation, Marriage, Ordination of Priests and the
Last Anointing. Although its foundation has an esoteric background as is true of all religions, the actual sacramental
community life as well as its proclamation of the Gospel in
accordance with the words of Christ Jesus in Matthew 28:19, is
exoteric.

This movement for religious renewal began in Germany,
Switzerland and Austria and then rapidly spread to Scandinavia,

Holland and Czechoslovakia. In 1929 it started in Britain. The first congregation was founded in the United States in 1948, and in Canada in 1952. Work in South Africa began in 1965, in Australia and New Zealand in 1988 and 1989. There are also congregations in Argentina, Belgium, Brazil, France, Ireland, Namibia, and Peru.

It is important to note that The Christian Community is *not* the 'religious wing' of the Anthroposophical Society. This idea represents a misunderstanding of both The Christian Community and Steiner's spiritual science. The Christian Community regards itself as a member of the invisible Church of Christ. and is intended as a renewal of the Christian Church itself. Anthroposophy, as Rudolf Steiner intended it, is concerned with the individual attainment of spiritual knowledge and the practical application of that knowledge to life.

The church of The Christian Community in Johannesburg.

A path to spiritual knowledge

Steiner defined anthroposophy as a path which can lead the *modern* human being to knowledge of higher worlds. He understood his work to be in the service of the spirit of our age, whom he named as the archangel Michael. Comparing his own work with the spiritual wisdom of an earlier age, Steiner said:

> Anthroposophy cannot be a revival of the Gnosis ... The work of anthroposophy is, by the light of Michael's agency, to evolve out of the spiritual soul a new form of understanding of Christ and the world. Gnosis was the old form of knowledge, preserved from earlier times — the one best able, at the time when the mystery of Golgotha took place, to convey this mystery to men's understanding.[44]

It was of the greatest importance for Steiner that his listeners and readers not simply hear his descriptions as a revelation to be accepted or rejected. We all have the responsibility today to know for ourselves. Of course, it may be necessary or even desirable to accept another's results as a tentative guide; Steiner said that thoughts and images which are correct can also serve to awaken within the listener or reader the ability to experience spiritual beings for himself. Steiner's descriptions were not intended as revelation in the dogmatic sense but to stimulate listeners to think on such matters in concrete detail. Such descriptions provide concepts which help us to see things which otherwise might not have been perceptible. Anthroposophy is meant to be enabling; dynamic not static, and therefore implicitly Christian because it stresses Becoming rather than Being. This dynamic, evolving conception of reality is seen in Steiner's understanding of angelic beings and even of God himself. Spiritual beings are themselves evolving; they progress by helping men and women, communities, nations and humanity as a whole, to evolve. True Christianity, understood as God's total solidarity with humanity achieved through Christ's taking on the fate of human beings, means that God himself is becoming, is growing, evolving and even increasing in goodness.

Steiner intended his teaching to help us, not simply to worship or fear spiritual beings, but to actually work consciously with them. Knowing the aims of God and his angelic hosts, knowing how they plan to achieve those goals enables us to work *with* them.

This knowing became possible because of Steiner's *method* of approach to esoteric knowledge. As we have seen it was a method founded essentially on the traditions of philosophic idealism of Middle Europe. In his hands this tradition made possible a genuine integration of the scientific spirit of the West and the world of the spirit realized when humanity crosses the threshold into the realms of mystical and occult experience. Only such an integration makes it possible for us to approach the hidden spiritual world without losing the greatest achievement of the West: the inner spiritual freedom that goes with clear, independent thinking. Christianity and Christian love will ultimately only survive and thrive on the earth to the extent that this inner spiritual freedom and clear, independent thinking becomes a part of our human being.

References

1. Steiner, *The Course of my Life,* p. 11.
2. Steiner, *The Course of my Life,* p. 24.
3. Steiner, *The Course of my Life,* p. 41.
4. Steiner, *The Course of my Life,* p. 274.
5. Variously published in English as *Truth and Knowledge* and *Truth and Science.*
6. *The Philosophy of Freedom,* p. 34.
7. Steiner, *The Course of My Life,* 1951, p. 276.
8. Indeed, seen from other perspectives, the human being can be described as seven, nine, or even twelvefold. Compare *Theosophy.*
9. Fichte, Johann Gottlieb, *The Science of Knowledge,* translated and edited by Peter Heath and John Lachs, Cambridge University Press, 1982, p. 98f.
10. There are three works by Herman Poppelbaum available in English which give a full account of Steiner's explanation of how evolution actually occurred and the nature of the relationship between Man and animal:
    Man and Animal: their Essential Difference, Anthroposophical Publishing Co, London 1960.
    New Light on Heredity and Evolution, St George Publications, New York 1977.
    A New Zoology, Philosophish-Anthroposophischer Verlag, Dornach 1961.
11. For a complete description of these beings' activities in nature see: Steiner, *Spiritual Beings in the Heavenly Bodies and in the Kingdoms of Nature.*
12. Steiner, *Exkurse in das Gebiet des Markus-Evangeliums,* Rudolf Steiner Verlag, Dornach, (Vol. 124 of collected works), p. 219 (author's own translation). Lecture of December 12, 1910.
13. Steiner, *The Gospel of St. John,* p. 108.
14. From Steiner, *Verses and Meditations,* p. 59.
15. *The Mystery of the Trinity and The Mission of The Spirit,* p. 96f. Lecture of July 30, 1922.
16. This quote comes from Fox's introduction to *Illuminations of*

Hildegard of Bingen, Bear & Company, Santa Fe, NM 1985. p. 12.

17. *From Jesus to Christ,* Lecture of October 7, 1911, p. 56.
18. For a very illuminating discussion of how Steiner's understanding of the process of human knowledge contains within it the essence of Christianity, death and Resurrection, see Frederick Hiebel's book, *The Epistles of Paul and Rudolf Steiner's Philosophy of Freedom,* St George Publications, New York 1980.
19. *The Gospel of St John,* p. 56ff.
20. For an interesting account of one such man see: Emil Bock, *The Three Years,* Chapter 1: 'Apollonius of Tyana and Jesus of Nazareth.'
21. The relationship between death and the Father God is discussed in Steiner's lecture cycle, *The Gospel of St John in its relation to the Other Three Gospels.*
22. *From Jesus to Christ.*
23. *From Jesus to Christ,* p. 69.
24. For Steiner's full account of how the Fall took place, how matter originated and the consequences for humankind in the form of the sickness of sin, see Steiner's lecture cycle, *The World of the Senses and the World of the Spirit.*
25. For a complete description of these beings' activities in nature see: Steiner, *Spiritual Beings in the Heavenly Bodies and in the Kingdoms of Nature.*
26. Steiner, *Christianity as Mystical Fact,* chapter titled 'The Apocalypse of John.'
27. For an excellent and detailed summary and study of Steiner's disclosures concerning the laws of karmic metamorphosis see: Guenther Wachsmuth, *Reincarnation as a Phenomenon of Metamorphosis,* Philosophic-Anthroposophic Press, Dornach 1961.
28. *The Philosophy of Freedom,* pp. 204ff.
29. See *Occult Science* for a description of the planetary incarnations of the earth and the inward, spiritual state between incarnations.
30. Steiner discusses this in his series of lectures *The Mission of the Individual Folk Souls.*
31. Boethius' book *The Consolation of Philosophy* is a moving account of just such visitations by this spiritual being known as Sophia.
32. *Über Philosophie, Geschichte und Literatur,* Rudolf Steiner

Verlag, Dornach 1983, (Vol. 51 of the collected works). Lecture held in Berlin, October 29, 1904, p. 203 (author's own translation).

33. *The Gospel of St John,* Lecture of May 31, 1908, p. 179.
34. See Hamburg lecture of May 30, 1908, contained in *The Gospel of St John.*
35. This theme is developed in Sergei O. Prokofieff's book *Eternal Individuality, Towards a Karmic Biography of Novalis,* Temple Lodge, London 1992. See Chapter 12, 'Christ and Sophia.'
36. Lecture of April 9, 1924, in *Karmic Relationships,* Vol. VI.
37. Steiner, *Luzifer-Gnosis,* 1903–08, Rudolf Steiner Verlag, Dornach (Vol. 34 of the collected works), p. 273 (author's own translation).
38. Steiner, *Die Mission der neuen Geistesoffenbarung,* Rudolf Steiner Verlag, Dornach (Vol. 127 of the collected works), p. 23 (author's own translation).
39. Steiner, *Die Mission der neuen Geistesoffenbarung.*
40. Steiner, *Bausteine zu einer Erkenntnis des Mysteriums von Golgatha,* Rudolf Steiner Verlag, Dornach (Vol. 175 of the collected works), Lecture of February 20, 1917, p. 56 (author's own translation).
41. Steiner, *Knowledge of the Higher Worlds,* p. 111.
42. Steiner, *The Gospel of St John,* p. 23.
43. Steiner, *Supersensible Influences in the History of Mankind,* pp. 48ff.
44. Steiner, *The Michael Mystery,* Vol.II of *Letters to the Members of the Anthroposophical Society.* Trans. E. Bowen-Wedgwood. 2nd edition, revised by George Adams. Anthroposophical Society, London 1956, p. 140.

Further reading

The following are considered Steiner's basic books:
(The volume number of Steiner's collected works, the German *Gesamtausgabe,* is shown in brackets)

The Philosophy of Spiritual Activity also known as *The Philosophy of Freedom,* Steiner Press, London 1964. New translation published as *Intuitive Thinking as a Spiritual Path: A Philosophy of Freedom.* New York 1995 (Vol. 4).

Theosophy: An Introduction to the Spiritual Processes in Human Life and the Cosmos, Anthroposophic Press, New York 1994 (Vol. 9).

How to Know Higher Worlds: A Modern Path of Initiation, Anthroposophic Press, New York 1994 (Vol. 10).

Occult Science: An Outline, Steiner Press, London 1979. Also published as *An Outline of Occult Science,* Anthroposophic Press, New York 1972 (Vol. 13).

Christianity as Mystical Fact and the Mysteries of Antiquity, Steiner Press, London 1972 (Vol. 8).

The Course of my Life, Anthroposophic Press, New York, 1951, 1986. Also published as *Rudolf Steiner, An Autobiography,* Steinerbooks, New York 1977 (Vol. 28).

Truth and Knowledge or *Truth and Science,* Steinerbooks, New York 1981 (Vol. 3).

Two important books revised from lectures:

The Spiritual Guidance of the Individual and Humanity, Anthroposophic Press, New York 1992 (Vol. 15).

The Redemption of Thinking, Anthroposophic Press, New York 1983 (Vol. 74).

The following lecture cycles presume a basic knowledge of Steiner's terminology developed in the above basic books:

The Gospel of St John, Anthroposophic Press, New York 1984 (Vol.104).

The Gospel of St Luke, Steiner Press, London 1968 (Vol. 114).

The Gospel of St Mark, Steiner Press, London and Anthroposophic Press, New York 1986 (Vol. 139).

The Gospel of St Matthew, Steiner Press, London and Anthroposophic Press, New York 1986 (Vol. 123).

The Gospel of St John and Its Relation to the Other Three Gospels, particularly to the Gospel of St Luke, Anthroposophic Press, New York 1982 (Vol. 112).

The Apocalypse of St John: Lectures on the Book of Revelation, Steiner Press, London 1985 (Vol. 104).

Background to the Gospel of St Mark, Steiner Press, London and Anthroposophic Press, New York 1985 (Vol. 124).

The Bhagavad Gita and the Epistles of Paul, Anthroposophic Press, New York 1971 (Vol. 142).

Building Stones for an Understanding of the Mystery of Golgotha, Steiner Press, London (Vol.175).

Christ and the Spiritual World: The Search for the Holy Grail, Steiner Press, London 1983 (Vol. 149).

The Christ Impulse and the Development of Ego Consciousness, Anthroposophic Press, New York 1976 (Vol. 116).

Christ in the Twentieth Century, Steiner Press, London 1973 (Vol. 131).

From Jesus to Christ, Steiner Press, Sussex 1991 (Vol. 131).

From Buddha to Christ, Anthroposophic Press, New York 1978.

The Fifth Gospel, Steiner Press, London 1985 (Vol. 148).

The Mission of the Archangel Michael, Steiner Press, London 1961 (Vol. 194).

The Pre-Earthly Deeds of Christ, Steiner Book Centre, North Vanouver 1979.

The Reappearance of Christ in the Etheric, Anthroposophic Press, New York 1983.

Three Streams in the Evolution of Mankind: The Connection of the Luciferic-Ahrimaic Impulses with the Christ-Jahve Impulse, Steiner Press, London 1985 (Vol. 184).

Verses and Meditations, Steiner Press, Bristol 1993.

Spiritual Beings in the Heavenly Bodies and in the Kingdoms of Nature, Anthroposophic Press, NewYork 1992 (Vol. 136).

The Mystery of the Trinity and The Mission of The Spirit, Anthroposophic Press, New York 1991 (Vol. 214).

The World of the Senses and the World of the Spirit, Steiner Book Centre, North Vancouver 1979 (Vol. 134).

The Mission of the Individual Folk Souls in Relation to Teutonic Mythology, Steiner Press, London 1970 (Vol. 121).

Karmic Relationships, Vol. VI, Steiner Press, London 1989 (Vol. 240).

Supersensible Influences in the History of Mankind, Rudolf Steiner Publishing Co, London 1956 (Vol. 216).

Books by other authors:

Barfield, Owen *Saving the Appearances: A Study in Idolatry.*

Benesch, Friedrich *Ascension,* Floris Books, Edinburgh 1979.

—, *Easter,* Floris Books, Edinburgh 1981.

—, *Whitsun: Community in the Age of Individualism,* Floris Books, Edinburgh 1979.

Bittleston, Adam *Our Spiritual Companions: From Angels and Archangels to Cherubim and Seraphim,* Floris Books, Edinburgh 1980.

Blattman, George *Radiant Matter: Decay and Consecration,* Floris Books, Edinburgh 1983.

Bock, Emil *The Apocalypse of St John,* Floris Books, Edinburgh 1986.

—, *Genesis: Creation and the Patriarch,* Floris Books, Edinburgh 1983.

—, *Kings and Prophets,* Floris Books, Edinburgh 1989.

—, *Moses,* Floris Books, Edinburgh 1986.

—, *St Paul,* Floris Books, Edinburgh 1993.

—, *The Three Years: the Life of Christ between Baptism and Ascension,* Floris Books, Edinburgh 1987.

Frieling, Rudolf *Christianity and Islam: a Battle for the True Image of Man,* Floris Books, Edinburgh 1980.

—, *Christianity and Reincarnation,* Floris Books, Edinburgh 1977.

—, *Hidden Treasures in the Psalms,* Christian Community Press, London 1967.

—, *Old Testament Studies,* Floris Books, Edinburgh 1987.

—, *The Essence of Christianity,* Floris Books, Edinburgh 1990.

Heidenreich, Alfred *Growing Point: The Story of the Foundation of The Christian Community,* Floris Books, Edinburgh 1979.

—, *Healings in the Gospels,* Floris Books, Edinburgh 1980.

Lauenstein, Diether *Biblical Rhythms in Biography,* Floris Books, Edinburgh 1983.

Madsen, Louise *The Christian Community, an Introduction,* Floris Books, Edinburgh 1995.

Prokofieff, Sergei O. *Eternal Individuality,* Temple Lodge, London 1992.

—, *The Spiritual Origins of Eastern Europe and the Future Mysteries of the Holy Grail,* Temple Lodge, London 1993.

Rittelmeyer, Friedrich *Meditation: Letters on the Guidance of the Inner Life, according to the Gospel of St John,* Floris Books, Edinburgh 1987.

—, *Reincarnation in the Light of Thought, Religion and Ethics,* Floris Books, Edinburgh 1988.

—, *Rudolf Steiner Enters My Life,* Floris Books, Edinburgh 1982.

Schroeder, Hans-Werner *The Christian Creed, A Meditative Path,* Floris Books, Edinburgh 1985.

Schütze, Alfred *The Enigma of Evil,* Floris Books, Edinburgh 1978.

Welburn, Andrew *The Beginnings of Christianity,* Floris Books, Edinburgh 1991.

Photographic acknowledgments

Classic Collection (pp.38, 49, 67, 68, 73, 84); Verlag am Goetheanum (pp.8, 18, 40); Hulton Deutsch Collection Ltd (pp.17, 21, 23, 29); Macallan Agency (pp.36, 46, 64, 70, 75, 78); Scala (pp.35, 56, 87); Weimar Archive (p.24).

Index